rhadamanthus

rHADA-mAnthuS

A Revenge Tragedy In Five Acts

WILL MADDEN

SQUARE STRAW PRESS
Washington, DC

Copyright © 2020 by Will Madden

Cover design by Amanda Lee Franck
afranck.myportfolio.com

All rights reserved. This book or any portion thereof may not be reproduced or used in any manner whatsoever without the express written permission of the publisher except for the use of brief quotations in a book review.

Printed in the United States of America

First Printing, 2020

ISBN 978-0-9981404-8-3
Square Straw Press
Washington, DC

"Seems," madam? Nay, it is. I know not "seems."
—*William Shakespeare,* Hamlet *(1.2.79)*

And art thou come, Horatio, from the depth,
To ask for justice in this upper earth?
To tell thy father thou art unreveng'd? . . .
For here's no justice. Gentle boy, begone;
For justice is exiled from the earth. . . .
Thy mother cries on righteous R[h]adamant
For just revenge against the murderers.
—*Thomas Kyd,* The Spanish Tragedie *(3.13)*

DRAMATIS *personæ*

RANDALL FLYNN: Impresario of the Mountebank Theater

RICO DAGGETT: A crooner, rumored to have killed his wife

PHILIP HUMPHREY: His valet

SERGIO PACK: An actor at the Mountebank

SAMSON LOOGEY: Ganglord and owner of an aluminum factory

LOUIS TENANT: His lieutenant

NOODLE: An enforcer for Loogey

BILLY PARLIAMENT: Labor organizer

TED C. HORNET: Newspaper reporter

VICTORIA SCHMUTZ: Television interviewer

NARRATOR: Voiceover on a documentary

2 GOONS: Aluminum industry thugs

Assorted cast of Hamlet (Claudius, Gertrude, ANNA as Ophelia, Laertes), stage crew, showgirls, photographers, reporters, party attendees (including director VIKTOR PLINKO), and an army of maniacal botanists

ACT one
SCENE one

(SETTING: The city of Dodoville in Sporqia, 1987. The head office of RANDALL FLYNN at the Mountebank Theater. The garish neon lighting of the outer facade is visible through the window. Mt Myrtle's volcanic dome fulminates further off in the night. Inside, the furniture and light fixtures befit a bank lobby. In the center of the far wall hangs an oversized human skull, jeweled and agape in laughter.)

(AT RISE: SERGIO PACK and RANDALL FLYNN play at billiards with PHILIP HUMPHREY in attendance. SERGIO, 30, is in costume as Hamlet from a performance earlier in the evening. FLYNN, mid-50s, wears a crisp charcoal gray shirt with a crimson handkerchief in the breast pocket. Of smallish stature, he possesses wiry strength and an assured posture. His circlet of graying hair remains in the disarray of one who has just risen from bed. HUMPHREY, late 40s, wears servant's attire with a slightly feminine cut. Horn-rimmed glasses hang from his breast pocket.)

(FLYNN chalks a pool cue with three deft strokes. As his leathery right hand crushes the red felt of the bumper, the cue indicates his call with sharp precision: snap, this ball, snap, this pocket, the tip looming over the precise center of each. With each move, SERGIO imagines he hears the stick whoosh. As FLYNN addresses his shot, a grandfather clock chimes twice. As the tolling dies away, FLYNN shoots, his touch soft on the cue. The target ball hangs on the lip of the pocket, as if choosing whether or not to fall. It does. FLYNN almost sneers. SERGIO, who notices HUMPHREY watching him, gestures for permission to smoke a cigarette. HUMPHREY shakes his head discreetly but emphatically no. FLYNN now misses an easy shot, clearing away a ball practically already in pocket. SERGIO mutters as he finds himself all snookered up. As he lines up his shot, FLYNN hovers too close behind him.)

FLYNN
(Voice raspy throughout)

Retribution, Pack, served cold. You are now an actor in a revenge play. Essentially, it's a simple part, based upon an elegant principle: for every action, an equal and opposite reaction.

rhadamanthus

SERGIO
(Scratching his shot)
It's bad science to apply nature's laws to the social sphere.

FLYNN
(Smiling)
Oh, but it's pleasurable! We like to believe truths are symmetrical in this way. Thirteen years ago, Rico Daggett murdered his wife, Mara Carpenter. Tomorrow night, he will die. Not merely just, but beautiful: he took a life, now his is taken away.

SERGIO
That's your idea of beauty? Blood for blood?

FLYNN
Yes. It's an economy of action: men commit crimes, then they pay for them. One of the many cycles perpetuated by nature: light and darkness, growth and decay. Crime and punishment, murder and retribution. Everyone has a role in it, we are all players.
(Lining up his next shot)
And tomorrow you will take center stage.

SERGIO
I'm only an actor, Mr. Flynn.

FLYNN
Then this is the opportunity you've been waiting for
(Striking the cue hard, sinking a striped ball)
to prove you can act decisively, as need requires.

SERGIO
A stage actor.

FLYNN

(As if this is his favorite subject)

The crooner, Rico Daggett: a man of appetites, of passions and addictions. While his wife lived, the tabloids were rank with stories of their marital strife. And then, while sailing off Majorca in their yacht, the famous actress was lost at sea. Upon his return, Daggett attributed Mara's death to . . . attack by giant jellyfish! A claim so bizarre, only an imbecile would forgo further scrutiny. Yet the state quickly ruled it an accident and closed the investigation. As public outcry grew louder to learn the truth, Rico Daggett fled the country. Like a fugitive of justice.

(Lines up a long shot)

Then, after ten years, he returns! And because he claims to have spent the intervening time starving and groveling like a monk, he is welcomed back to Dodoville as a reformed sinner. He still comports himself like a guilty man, yet once again the machine of law does not move.

(He shoots. This ball also lingers upon the lip of the
pocket before it, too, falls.)

In an age when justice's hand is stilled, it must fall to private citizens to pick up the sword the courts have laid down.

(Offers the cue to SERGIO)

SERGIO

(Backing away)

The boating accident was a long time ago. Perhaps he really is reformed. The famous temper, at least, seems to have abated.

FLYNN

I am not a hard man. Let salvation be yet the wage of repentance; but for hypocrisy, the sword of justice must not be removed. Do not be fooled by the *du*plicity of *pub*licity: Daggett has never atoned for murdering Mara Carpenter. Just as he betrayed their marriage in life, he now disgraces her memory in death. Upon the same stage where you performed tonight, Daggett exploits her tragedy in a manner which not only reveals his guilt, but would condemn him even if he were innocent.

SERGIO

To be fair, Mr. Flynn, you put him on that stage.

FLYNN

I did. Since the state prosecutor would not lay the case before the people, I have done it for him. I have stood Daggett before the whole world and given him opportunity to account for the loss of his wife at sea—what was it?—"under unascertainable circumstances" thirteen years ago. Three nights a week, he trembles on stage and weeps for Mara's return. Seven nights a week, he debauches himself with booze and women to make the devil blush!

(Trembling with anger)

He mocks her memory, Pack!

(Standing beside FLYNN, HUMPHREY nods in agreement.)

SERGIO

Memory-mocking is not actually a crime.

FLYNN

(His nostrils flaring)

Is it justice then, that after tomorrow night, after that crescendo of obscenity planned for his farewell performance, he should retire to peace and comfort?

(Glances at HUMPHREY, who stiffens)

SERGIO

(Timidly)

No.

will madden

FLYNN

Mara Carpenter's death was ruled an accident. So be it. Accidents can happen to anybody. After the show, Daggett will return to his room at the Norway Hotel. You will make sure he takes his sleeping pill—perhaps the only thing which permits his filthy conscience to rest!—then you will burn the room down around him. Humphrey will show you how to make it look careless, as if he dozed off with a lit cigarette and ignited the sheets. Since he killed with water, it will be by flame that he passes to the everlasting bonfire. It is symmetrical, Pack.

SERGIO
(Trying to sound assertive)
Symmetry doesn't make anything right.

FLYNN

But it gets people's attention! We are about to embark upon a whole purge of accidents, you and I. The death of Rico Daggett will be but the first among this city's malefactors. Next, we will punish those whose backroom dealings destroyed our industries, who ground down its peace and prosperity into mob rule and street horror. Then, I will bring down the profiteers who gave our nation over to defeat and humiliation in war at the hands of the Zahz. Tomorrow night will put Dodoville on notice: that Justice is not dead, that her sword will flash, if needs be, in unsanctioned hands.
(Looking down at his palms)
Over the years, I have gathered up Dodoville's most corrupt, baiting my palm as you would a mousetrap. The time has finally come to crush them all. I will have the satisfaction of hearing the bones crack and feeling the flesh squish, of allowing the hot blood to congeal upon my skin.

rhadamanthus

SERGIO

(Under his breath)

Jesus.

FLYNN

Rico Daggett will be the first. Thirteen years! Like Faust, he has exhausted the liberty of his contracted term, and now the devil comes to claim him. And you will be hell's bailiff, Pack. You will carry forth the sword from the abyss.

SERGIO

I . . .

FLYNN

And you will do this on account of another symmetry—in exchange for the great favor I have done for you. It was I who designed the stage production which has made your name overnight. I have plucked you from obscurity and placed you as a headliner on the same stage as the greatest entertainment talents of our age. In me, you have found the chariot which draws your star to the pinnacle of heaven.

SERGIO

(Aside)

Ah me, I've beseeched hell, and now Rhadamanthus demands his due!

FLYNN

And so it now falls to your hand to slay a befouled man, who throughout his life has paid no tithe to Fortune for the gifts she has bestowed upon him. Because of his honeyed voice, doors open to him without lifting a hand to knock. Without toiling, he is invited to every table. The ten years which Rico Daggett lived in exile, the public has accepted as the debt he's paid to society—as if he spent it in prison and not some tropical paradise! Is this justice: for *murder* to suffer temporary severance from Dodoville's blind adoration?

      (SERGIO appeals to HUMPHREY, who again shakes his head.)

No. Let a man sing for his dinner, but not his salvation. The soul demands something more to make heaven its just desert.

SERGIO

    (Aside)

How can I deny him and keep the stage? Or my head?

FLYNN

You must do this, Pack. The state will not prosecute him. The state is the crime!

SERGIO

    (Aside)

My heart's conflicted, but my mouth can make only one answer.
    (To FLYNN)
I'll do as you say.

FLYNN

Good. Humphrey will instruct you. Know your part in this perfectly by tomorrow night.

      (Exit SERGIO. HUMPHREY exchanges a glance with FLYNN before putting on his glasses and following.)

                           (BLACKOUT)

SCENE two

(SETTING: Morning. RICO DAGGETT's dressing room.)

(AT RISE: DAGGETT nurses a hangover as he sits in the stylist's chair. HUMPHREY, wearing glasses, cuts his hair. DAGGETT, in his early 60s, looks his age and more, his hair and eyebrows dyed an unconvincing black.)

DAGGETT
Easy with my head, Humphrey. It feels like a cannon went off in there.

HUMPHREY
More grappa than grapeshot, I think, Mr. Daggett. I warned you, didn't I, sir?

DAGGETT
Cork the devil's ass with your warnings!
      (A knock without)
Speaking of.

(Enter TED C. HORNET in a striped seersucker suit. The press pass worn in the ribbon of his hat, a cinematic convention elsewhere, is standard practice in Sporqia.)

God's gracious wrath! Good morning, Ted.

HORNET
(With a Golden Age of Hollywood accent)
Never thought you'd see the sun shine on this day, did you, Rick?

DAGGETT
(Wincing as he shakes his head no)
Thought my heart would have given out long ago.

HORNET
Not a heart as big and strong as yours!

DAGGETT
Old and weary. Don't start believing your own lies. There's some cherries on the table, I had Humphrey pit them for you.

HORNET
I just ate a big breakfast.

DAGGETT
Have some anyway, they're poisoned.

HORNET
Thank you, no.

DAGGETT
Poisonous, like those eels in my act!

rhadamanthus

HORNET

I believe that is only a rumor. I'm told they like people.

DAGGETT

But what about me? Do they like *me*? Oh, the things I'd tell you if.

HORNET

If what?

DAGGET

If I was people. I'd tell you of the rickety platform I gotta ride as I sing above that eel tank—I'm just as terrified as I was the first night. How the wood creaks and shakes. Of the dizzy height I dangle above the water, and, Christ on a cracker, of how I fall to my knees just to lower my center of gravity. In case of strong wind, indoors or no! Ted, I'd tell you these things if you promised they stayed here.

HORNET
(Taking a seat across from DAGGETT)
But that would be a lie, Ricky!

DAGGETT

Well, that's news. So to speak.
(Eats one of the cherries)
What I say instead is, I am just as filled with emotion out there. As day one.

HORNET

Fear is an emotion. Any others the people ought to know about?

DAGGETT

Before I answer, do you mind telling me if you've already finished writing this well-worded, factual article for tomorrow's paper?

will madden

HORNET

May depend upon your answers.

DAGGETT

Because this is excruciating. Emotion? These days, I try not to feel more than I have to.

HORNET

It's in your contract to feel things, Mr. Daggett. To feel them for the *Spyhole*. Especially on red-letter days like today. Your final performance at the Mountebank Theater.

DAGGETT

(With fake enthusiasm)

All these special guests! People who've been with me since the beginning. Caboose LaShane, Andy Penult, Pescadeux LaSponk, Tabatha Crispin. Also, the Shandy Pipers, Rose Hawthorne, Or'nge Marlon, "Porqi" al-Rashir, and the Joywright Trio. All these people I never met till a week ago. Still don't know which one Marlon is.

HORNET

I've seen the press release. And he's the one with the chin.

DAGGETT

I shouldn't be speaking to you. To save my voice.

HORNET

Now Ricky, tonight you could crow like a rooster for two hours, the crowd would weep right through it. You know as well as anyone.

DAGGETT

Still, there's something to say for artistry.

rhadamanthus

HORNET

Why don't you tell me what it is, Rick? On the record.

DAGGETT

I never should have allowed Flynn to lure me out of retirement. How he found me, I still don't know. A snowy little village in the Andes I scarcely knew the name of. I come home one night, someone's in my kitchen frying bananas. "Shut the door," he says, "there's a draft." That's when I recognize him, the crackpot who used to stand in Krompachy Park on Sunday afternoons and beat the lamppost with a big aluminum bell. Figure he's here to actually carry out one of the insane sentences he used to hand down to the city's ganglords to make people laugh. Instead, he has a business proposition. I've never heard of a more sinister contract—and I'm in show business!

HORNET

Remember, I don't speak legal.

DAGGETT

Did you know Flynn is shelling out a lump sum for these performances at the end of my engagement, but that I forfeit the entire payment should I fail to appear for a single show? No exceptions: illness, kidnapping, trapped by lava flow. That I'm under a gag order not to mention this clause to anyone?

HORNET

I respect your privacy.

DAGGETT

Not even going to make a note of it, are you? In case of incident?

HORNET

Fine print is so confusing.

will madden

DAGGETT

(Sighing)

Anyways, for three years, I've been back in Dodoville, where they drink the blood of a dying man. I love these people! That's my emotion, put it. After the greatest tragedy of my life—helpless to watch my wife drown—I am terrified of water, by the way—they wanted to impale my head on a pike. Did you know someone hammered a kitten to the door of my hotel room? Iron nail right through the eye socket. "You next" written above, in case I didn't get it. Mind you, this the same town where Rupert Khan threw his political rival out a sixth story window.

HORNET

Not that again, please.

DAGGETT

Right onto a busy sidewalk. People had to leap out of the way! Rupert pokes his head through the broken glass and what's he say? "And stay out!" This man still won the next election.

HORNET

That was a different era.

DAGGETT

Me who suffered tragedy, he has to go into exile, disgraced and fearing for his life. I'm in this tiny mountain village not even horses can reach, scrutinizing every face I see. 'Cause when I left, rumor was I had a bounty on my head! Then Flynn hogties me back here. A mob meets at the airport—and I swear to God it's the same one that drove me off—only now they're demanding to be loved. Like nothing ever happened. "O Rico, Rico, how's your trip? Rico, when you gonna sing again for us? O sole sole, la la la." "My people," I say to them, "oh I missed you all so much!" Tears in my eyes. Real tears, 'cause any minute they might tear me apart on the tarmac.

rhadamanthus

HORNET

(Not listening)

Sounds very dramatic.

DAGGETT

And it hasn't let up. Three years of this now, never knowing what kind of crazy is coming at me. These are my feelings. Put 'em. In the newspaper, please. About me gonna miss the people of Dodoville.

HORNET

The *Spyhole*'s reading public is above criticism, Rick. And I didn't hear a word about artistry, if you want the truth.

DAGGETT

The truth, and—only 'cause this interview's exclusive—the *Dodoville Spyhole* crucified me the worst. Of all the daily rags. Both times, on the coming and the going.

HORNET

Excruciating. Crucified. Do you consider yourself a Christ figure, Rick?

DAGGETT

Fuck you, Ted. "The most comprehensive coverage of my career." Put that too, I said it.

HORNET

Already have.

DAGGETT

Edward C. Hornet, prescient pen.

HORNET

I like the ring, can I put it on my cards?

                              DAGGETT

You're asking permission?

                              HORNET

No.

                              DAGGETT

Speaking of prescience, I'm going to proceed as if I already know what you are going to ask.

                              HORNET

I'd prefer it at this stage. Saves my breath.

                              DAGGETT

Thirteen years ago when my wife died in that dreadful boating accident, the world accused me of killing her. And although nothing connected me to her death besides being there, I fled this city. I fled the hounding of the press, especially that one piece of filth, what's it called? Ah, yes, the Spyhole.

                              HORNET

Tut.

                              DAGGETT

Shush, it's therapeutic. I fled the harassment of strangers in the street, I fled my own shame over not being able to save her. But to the whole world it appeared I had fled justice. That's why I felt it necessary to return. This city already knows I am a man of many faults, but why permit them to add cowardice to the list?

                              HORNET

I have all this on file already, Rick. Practically verbatim.

rhadamanthus

DAGGETT

Ted, my hate for you burns with the heat of a thousand hells. Some days I wonder if you aren't my closest friend. What does that say about me?

HORNET

Extraordinary things. Maybe nothing.

DAGGETT

Do you consider us two friends?

HORNET

Of course I do, Rick!

DAGGETT

Here's one you can print. I'm going to fucking kill you. Lance your head to a pole so your toes just barely don't touch the ground. Jaw hung open like I caught you by surprise.

HORNET

A terrific front-page photo! Honestly, Rick, my editor could make it happen. I hope this doesn't get back to her.

DAGGETT

Do you really hope?

HORNET

A little, at least.

DAGGETT

This is how much I hate you, Ted. I'm going to leave you in your misery.

HORNET

(A sad smile)

Right back at you, pally.

DAGGETT

Here's me still talking. I did a lot of private grieving during those years abroad, but I realized I could never heal until I sang my dirges, all my songs of midnight longing in public, before the city whose gaze I've held my whole life long. Now I'm going to sing that awful song at you again, you piece of shit.

HORNET

Hit me with it. "This reporter was serenaded with a private performance by the legendary crooner." I can put it if it's true.

DAGGETT

Apparently, you can put it if it's not! From the devil's ass to your ear.

(Sings)

O where are you my Mara
Whom all the world adored
The girl I loved my Mara
Hair strewn upon the shore

Come back my darling Mara
Come back from the sea
I'll go back to Mara
If she comes not back to me

HORNET

I'd have said this even if it wasn't true: that was really moving, Rick.

DAGGETT

When I began this engagement, I didn't think I could handle that song three nights a week for three years. "To Mara" and "To Mara" and "To Mara." But over time, the terrible pun became endearing to me, that little self-mocking turn made catharsis possible. It taught me that although my sins have been serious,

rhadamanthus

I had no obligation to take myself seriously. I could laugh at myself. Bitterly at first, and then. Well, still bitterly.

HORNET

I hope you don't expect me to print any of that.

DAGGETT

(Pulling his face)

My brow grows heavy, the skin sags, the hair silvers.

HORNET

Absolute trash, Rick. I'm sorry.

DAGGETT

I'm quoting you! Those were your words, front page! Day after opening night, 24 August, 1984.

HORNET

I hope you're proud of yourself.

DAGGETT

Talking. I'm looking forward to after tonight, leaving the lights and cameras and crowds behind. I'm gonna lead a humble life. As in near the earth. Growing up in New Guernsey, I helped my grandfather tend a little vegetable garden. Somewhere in this ol' noggin, I've stowed away knowledge of how to draw sustenance from the soil. I will care for carrots. I will make my peace by growing peas.

HORNET

(Getting up to leave)

Eloquent. My heart stills.

DAGGETT
Any chance of it making copy? I doubt you can do better!

HORNET
Already have. Go out and have a great show tonight, Rick.

DAGGETT
(Superstitious)
That's not what you are supposed to say! In a theater, you know? Especially not this one.

HORNET
It's what you say if you're me.

DAGGETT
I'll miss you, Ted. That's a truth you can print.

HORNET
Is it?
(HORNET exits.)

DAGGETT
Well, don't get sentimental! Humphrey, that man does not care for me.

HUMPHREY
(Still cutting hair)
Oh, I don't know about that, sir.

DAGGETT
He thinks he's better than me, and—I don't want to throw this in his face but—excuse me, he's a journalist. Nobody's more debased than that, are they?

HUMPHREY
(Grimly)
I'm sure it's possible.

rhadamanthus

DAGGETT
Lawyers, maybe.

HUMPHREY
I couldn't say which is better or worse.

DAGGETT
You? No, of course, you couldn't. The point is, I won't complain about getting lumped with lawyers or journalists. But below them? Extreme, isn't it?

HUMPHREY
It's not my business to say.

DAGGETT
I'm not asking you a business question, Humphrey. What do you *think?* Would you mix us all in the same pot?

HUMPHREY
Not a stew I'd eat at any rate.

DAGGETT
(Puffs his cheeks then sighs)
My career ends tonight, I'm feeling ruminative. Decades of success and failures, triumphs and humiliations. In a few hours, it's over. Forever. More than a man can process.

HUMPHREY
Everyone believes you'll sing again, sir.
(Time passes.)

DAGGETT
It's more than my career that's over, isn't it?
(He turns in the chair to gaze behind him.)
Humphrey.

HUMPHREY

I'm not sure what you mean.

DAGGETT

I mean, for three years Flynn's been building up my story to a climax, and not even Halavah Torres and his full orchestra will cut it. Time for the coup de grace.

HUMPHREY

Is that French, sir?

DAGGETT

It might be. Some of these people think I'm a hero, others the devil himself. Either way, it's time for the curtain, yes? Big satisfying finish?

HUMPHREY

(Brightly)

A farewell concert. Yes, sir.

DAGGETT

No. Flynn's an impresario, but not of just the Mountebank. His stage is the whole city. And there's no way I get off it alive, is there?

HUMPHREY

(With inappropriate lightness)

I don't know, sir.

DAGGETT

(Irritated)

I'm not asking for clairvoyance here, just your opinion. Doesn't it seem that's how it'll play out?

rhadamanthus

HUMPHREY
(Dispenses shaving foam for the back of DAGGETT's neck)
I still don't know.

DAGGETT
Who do you think it'll be?

HUMPHREY
Who what'll be?

DAGGETT
(Watching HUMPHREY strop the razor in the mirror)
I can't decide if I want to see it coming. Part of me wants to stare death in the eye and say I'm not afraid. But mostly, I don't want to see it coming. Anyways, if you were Flynn, who would you send to do the job?

HUMPHREY
Me, sir? I wouldn't *send* anybody.

DAGGETT
No, because you take orders. I used to think you were Flynn's spy. Well, because you're Flynn's spy. So I gave you useless shit to do just make your life miserable. And you did it, exactly as I asked. This was when we first started. Do you remember?

HUMPHREY
I'm sure I don't know what you mean.

DAGGETT
Meaning, you don't know what I asked just to break balls, and what because I was high as a kite.

HUMPHREY

Are those things different, sir?

DAGGETT

We've been through a lot together, us two. I won't say I've been good to you, it'd be a lie. But you've always been there. Flynn wanted to break me on that stage. He broke me. Somebody else might have used prayer or mediation to get through it. Not me. Booze, drugs, women. I'm not extraordinary like that. I've treated lots of people badly. I treated you badly. But you've gotta know I've never been happy for a minute. Look at the press photos for Christ's sake, the smile can't look any more painted on. Humphrey, I know I haven't atoned for anything, only suffered. Eventually hollow pleasures become real pain. You know that, because you've been here to see it all. The slime trail I've left under all the paint.

HUMPHREY

(Shaves DAGGETT)

I've seen all there is to see, but I know no more than I know.

DAGGETT

(Frustrated)

In ten minutes, I have to go out and say what an honor it's been to perform at the Mountebank Theater, how proud I am to end my career where it began, in Dodoville, the greatest city in the world, before the greatest audience in the world. Then they'll applaud and I'll get puffed up on it, 'cause that's the whore I am. Tell me something real, Humphrey. Anything.

HUMPHREY

(Stops as if contemplating a choice)

I can honestly say I haven't been ordered to kill you.

rhadamanthus

DAGGETT

That's too bad. I wish it was you, because then we could talk some things over. Not talk you out of it, I don't mean that. If you were ordered, I know I couldn't bribe you. You're a goddamn machine, Humphrey. Take that as a compliment if you like, 'cause I mean it that way. But maybe you'd hold my hand as I died. That wouldn't be against the rules.

>(Imitating FLYNN)

Let the blade be merciless, not you.

>(Smiles)

Maybe not comfort me, maybe that's too much. But stay in the room at least. Watch. Know when I've gone. If I need to die, sure, fine. God knows I've had my share of chances. But die alone, who profits?

>(Waits in vain for a response)

So maybe you could manage that. We've spent most of every day together for three years, you're almost a stranger to me. That's the death I would choose for myself. No hooch, no broads, no tra la la. Just you and me, an intimate setting, like this. No witnesses, no fuss.

>(DAGGETT grips the arm of his chair and closes his
>eyes. After a pregnant pause, HUMPHREY cleans
>the razor and puts it away.)

Is that the best you can do with my hair? I have to go out in five minutes and lie to people.

HUMPHREY

You're the one who doesn't trust professional barbers, sir.

DAGGETT

A professional barber wouldn't nick me a tenth as often.

HUMPHREY

>(With a hint of a smile)

Undoubtedly true, sir.

DAGGETT

Humphrey, you're my valet, so there's something I need to tell you. I know I can't step off that stage tonight if I want to live, so I've decided not to get on it. I'm going to disappear before the curtain goes up.

HUMPHREY
(Without surprise or concern)

Impossible, sir. Everyone's expecting you.

DAGGETT

Let 'em wait till doomsday. Halavah Torres can do the show. They don't need me at all. Just play the music, those people will sing the songs themselves. That's how it is some nights, two hours of me mostly listening to them. "O sole sole."

(Suddenly angry)

So let them give the concert! 'Cause if I'm not out of the country by morning . . . It's only a matter of time.

HUMPHREY

It's my job to make sure you appear on stage tonight. As it is every night. If you're breathing, sir, out you go.

DAGGETT

If I'm breathing. To you, it seems like cowardice to run. Are you kidding? It's the brave thing. Facing death doesn't scare me half as much as living in solitude again. This exit will mean I can never come back. That's important. The hypocrites, the opportunists, the sycophants. I can't live without them. Ever since I was a choir boy at St Ambrose's, I've had to make people love me. The days I despise them most are the days I work the hardest. I'm disappointed when they don't demand more of me.

rhadamanthus

HUMPHREY

(Casually)

Running *is* the brave thing, sir. That's why you won't do it.

DAGGETT

(Shouting)

Put Flynn on notice, I'm a flight risk!

HUMPHREY

No need, sir. I have it handled.

DAGGETT

Well, you've been warned.

HUMPHREY

So have you, sir.

(CURTAIN)

ACT two
SCENE one

(SETTING: Video viewing room at the Mountebank Theater. A screen is lowered in front of the stage.)

(AT RISE: SERGIO PACK dressed as Hamlet enters from one of the aisles, inserts a videotape into the player, sits in the first row to view an old news reel: it's the Sporqia National News, SDOD Ch. 4. Recorded in the 1980s, but with color from an earlier era, washed out and cracked. Old-timey projection sounds. Cigarette burns in nonsensical places with increasing frequency. Overplay of medieval lute music.)

NARRATOR
(Nostalgic throughout)
The famous facade of Dodoville's Mountebank Theater

rhadamanthus

(Mountebank pictured on screen: the building only a model) widely decried as an eyesore when it opened in 1984. At night, the structure was said to resemble a corpse crawling up out of the River Dodos.

> (The theater's facade shown split-screen against a figure climbing out of a hot tub, giving a silent-film era cry, then passing out face down, legs still in the water)

The design is usually attributed to hometown architect, Pierre Takoberu

> (Takoberu shown in a black-and-white photo: a lanky man in Elizabethan dress smoking a corncob pipe, more-or-less stoically enduring a parrot bothering his hair)

who had died tragically in 1979.

> (The scene is rendered in Play-Doh: a man lies on his back at a construction site, a cinder block where his head should be. Forelegs cross-gartered, pipe in hand. One or two drops of blood visible. A construction worker faces the camera in Munch's Scream pose. A caption flashes in dramatic lettering: "RECREATION")

The following year, Randall "Rhadamanthus" Flynn acquired the site of the future theater, formerly an aluminum plant owned by the Loogey ganglord family.

> (Photo of Flynn in Panama hat and waistcoat, standing with his thumbs in his belt in front of a factory. Behind him, a "SOLD" sticker across the door. Above the threshold, the Loogey Industries logo: the Loogey name lettered in semi-circle around a water splash. Caption: 1980.)

The old factory core remains unmistakably present in the Mountebank design.

> (A sepia photo of the factory wipes to an over-color-corrected still of the Mountebank. The structures look nothing alike.)

Randall Flynn invested very little of his own money in the theater, and none of his backers were Sporqish.

> (70s color photograph of Flynn walking into a bar with three of his investors, each wearing a different national costume.)

Flynn convinced foreign backers that by injecting money into the old aluminum plant, they would position themselves at the forefront of the revamped industry model.

> (A still of Flynn standing with grinning shareholders, each holding up a different kind of aluminum siding)

He failed to mention that "revamped" meant novelty acts

> (Video: two men take turns malleting each other in the ankles. Dissolves into a ferret-legging competition.)

and showgirls.

> (A court dance sequence from a 1950s sword and sandal film. Cut to: Elderly Victora-era women standing motionless with a powerful fan on them)

The Zahzian War of 1982 slowed the renovation

> (Stills of WWI trenches intercut with sequences from 1960s science fiction laser battles)

but the Mountebank's chief obstacle was its location. Randall Flynn had built the theater in the heart of the Siding, the district home to Dodoville's aluminum industry until its collapse in the late 1970s. During the economic downturn, police had cracked down on union demonstrations

> (Chippendales performing in cop uniforms dodge drinks thrown at them)

rhadamanthus

while industry bosses dispatched notorious enforcers known as the Blackrings to subdue labor organizers.

>(Wet cement poured upon grocery-packaged pork chops)

The Siding quickly became the most brutal area of a town already renowned for violence and cruelty.

>(Two schoolchildren with a water balloon play keep-away from a man on fire. The man gives up, throwing his hat on the ground in frustration.)

As the Mountebank neared completion, many Dodoville residents swore they would never return to the Siding, even should the beloved Marcel Portmanteau

>(A man in white-face performs cliché racial parodies.)

promise to grant one final performance upon its stage before hurling himself directly into the lava lake atop Mount Myrtle.

>(A marshmallow man on a stick ignites over a campfire. Molten globs drip off into the flames.)

Dodovilleans feared muggers who might camp in nearby abandoned warehouses, waiting to ambush well-dressed theater-goers.

>(Silent-film style recreation: Two men stand at a window in Zforro masks, alternately twirling their mustaches and rubbing their palms together devilishly. The second man also rubs them over a fire for warmth.)

The first week, the Mountebank's marquee boasted no lesser talents than Freddy Indigo,

>(A blindfolded man throws knives at a woman turning upon a wheel. The man pivots suddenly and hurls a knife savagely at the camera.)

Agatha Sweetcorn,

> (A heavyset woman sits in a bathtub with a foam
> castle on her head, operating marionettes with her feet)

and Halavah Torres performing with his full orchestra.

> (A hobo clown plays the harp, backed by musicians in
> formal attire.)

But star-power alone would not yet lure a local audience to his theater. Early on, tickets were sold primarily to entertainment enthusiasts in Creston, who never heard about the horrors of Blackring enforcers. Upon seeing the abandoned factories and warehouses, cheapskate Crestonites preferred to brook the gates of hell than let the price of tickets go to waste.

> (A Creston burgher in a body cast gives broken-
> toothed smile and thumbs up.)

Many said if Rhadamanthus Flynn wanted to bring in a crowd, he'd have to kidnap an audience and strap them to the benches.

> (The camera pans over the Mountebank's empty
> seating, including a discount section where only the
> edge is provided)

In fact, a corralling did prove necessary. Taking a page from the old British Navy, Flynn had the Blackrings rounded up and impressed into maritime service.

> (Recreation: A man in a Zorro mask stops before an
> alleyway. A sign reads "FREE" above an image of a
> burlap sack with a dollar sign on it. Venturing down
> the alley, he is blackjacked, stuffed into a burlap sack,
> and thrown longwise into a wagon. As the
> kidnappers turn, a dollar sign is visible on the sack.)

They were crewed upon the cargo vessel *Unduly*, to bring back shipments of papaya from the Keenwall Islands.

> (Parchment map. A ship with a trailing dashed red
> line emerges from a question-marked cloud, does

> one loop-de-loop en route to an archipelago of islands shaped like a sad face.)

The *Unduly* went down a few miles south of the Tropic of Cancer with eighty-seven souls aboard.

> (An animated shark devours the ship off the map.)

With the Siding cleared out, Dodovilleans got over their fear of Blackrings and paid top dollar to watch their favorite stars perform.

> (Korvish MacAle, celebrity dentist, performs a particularly tricky root canal to thunderous acclaim.)

But what really drew them in was the wretched humiliations to which Rhadamanthus Flynn forced his performers to submit on stage.

> (Halavah Torres, clouded in a swarm of gnats, runs terrified as Agatha Sweetcorn chases him with a pail of her soapy bathwater.)

Humbling the proud had been Randall Flynn's trademark long before he became impresario of Dodoville's most lavish entertainment venue. In his younger days, he was known for standing in Krompachy Park and handing down draconian sentences upon prominent Dodovilleans.

> (Flynn shown in doorman's livery with veins popping on his forehead. He rings a large bell under the statue of an officer on horseback. His hair is a mess.)
>
> (Cut to: CLANCY LANCET shown in a tweed jacket, sitting on a folding chair in a school gymnasium, smoking a pipe. Sneakers squeak in the background. Throughout, an adult male voice can be heard berating someone called Chalky for a "sugar-bottomer's" lack of hustle.)

LANCET

In those days, Flynn was a doorman at the Wilhelm Voigt Hotel over in North Umbrage. On his days off, he used to dress in his liveries and wander down to

Krompachy Park, right in front of the statue of Colonel Gelding. I think he was pretending to be town crier at first, because he carried this giiiiant aluminum bell. People would ignore him, so he'd smash

> (Mimes passing a baton)

the bell against a pole, right next to somebody's head. Scared the bejevil out of 'em, you know. "Hear ye, hear ye," (this was him) "so-and-so has committed such-and-such egreeeegious crime and will paaaay the penalty!" People would say, "Hey look at this crackpot" . . . but they started egging him on! "Oh, yeah, what's this big penalty gonna be?" And Randy told them. In fact, he'd go into great detail. "Oh-h-h-h!" He'd roar like the old stage actors, you know. "A sword of purest silver"

> (Mimes holding a tall stack of paper cups)

"will pierce to the depth of his cirrhotic liver. Imps will cut off his eyelids and staple them over his butthole." Always very dramatic, very gory. Most people thought he was nuts, but everybody loved him. Big crowd every week.

> (Smiles artificially)

NARRATOR

When people asked Flynn when these sentences would be carried out, he'd say, "In hell if not in life." Marty Sturgis of the *Dodoville Spyhole* began to refer to Randall Flynn as "Rhadamanthus" in his editorials.

> (Cut to: MARTY STURGIS. CLANCY LANCET in
> a different wig. He sits in his office at an undersized
> desk. Sweat drenches his hairline and shirt. An
> oscillating desk fan sometimes obscures his voice. In
> the background, a woman can be heard berating a
> reporter called Chalky for not preferring the active voice.)

STURGIS

Rhadamanthus was one of the mythical judges of the underworld. There were three of them: Minos, Aeacus, and Rhadamanthus. In life, Minos was the

rhadamanthus

legendary ruler of Crete. You may know him from Dante's *Inferno*. Aeacus was master of the winds; he shows up in the *Odyssey* and *Aeneid*. Rhadamanthus was also is associated with Crete, but fewer people have heard of him. But Rhadamanthus is close to Randall, you see. Ruh-ruh-randall, Ruh-ruh-rhadamanthus. Nobody really got it first. In fact, everyone was confused. But I kept doing it, over and over and over. Nearly got me fired. Actually did, twice, actually. But eventually Randy heard about it. Well he liked it, sorta adopted it for himself. Which, good for me, it probably saved my career. Rhadamanthus! Jesus, I musta looked like a real jackass there for a while.

>(Smiles artificially)

NARRATOR

Randall Flynn exploited his reputation as an infernal judge by having famed entertainers at the Mountebank reenact their most painful and shameful experiences in their performances.

>(Pescadeux LaSponk grits his teeth as a bloomered 5-
>year-old bends over to pick flowers.)

Every crooner, comedian, and chorus girl who had cheated and backstabbed their way up in the industry paid for it at the Mountebank on the way down. But before their debut on stage, the local tabloids

>(Savage headlines shown from the *Spyhole*, the
>*Inquisitor*, and the *Parrot*)

printed takedown pieces on them, laying out past misdeeds in sordid detail. By the time they appeared on stage, the audience was a half-inch from a lynch mob.

>(Silhouettes of pitchforks in the audience obscure a
>nervous Monty Bedlam on stage)

By that era, Flynn had truly become an underworld dispenser of justice—at least in the entertainment industry, which more than satisfied the average tabloid reader.

>(Montage of stills from Mountebank performances)

will madden

For a few hours a night under those insane lights on the River Dodos, the old aluminum district was a kind of hell on earth. And Randall Flynn charged admission.

> (Flynn stands smiling outside a ticket booth with his hand out, the other fist holding three black hounds on a single leash.)

The celebrated entertainers to perform upon the Mountebank stage include Rico Daggett, whose wife died offshore in an alleged jellyfish attack

> (Photo of Daggett on a cruise ship scowling as Mara flirts with a porter)

and Sergio Pack

> (Pictured addressing the occipital bone of a skull in a graveyard)

whose name has been implicated in the gangland death of—

> (SERGIO turns off the projector and exits.)

(BLACKOUT)

SCENE two

(SETTING: Video viewing room at the Mountebank. Action will take place live behind the screen, which flashes intermittently with static.)

(AT RISE: DAGGETT walks into the viewing room, turns on the player, and sits in the front row. The video is of a local interview show called Inspiring People. The host is VICTORIA SCHMUTZ, a middle-aged woman with a haircut typical for a 1950s American sitcom, which her viewing audience considers fresh and edgy. She reads all her lines from a prompter, addressing them to the camera.)

VICTORIA
Our first guest tonight is one of Dodoville's most recognizable personalities. He is also the owner and operator of the city's newest and most astonishing

entertainment venue, the Mountebank Theater. Ding-a-ling, everybody, it's the incomparable Mr. Randall Flynn!

> (FLYNN enters wearing his charcoal gray slacks and dress shirt, red socks. In public, Flynn affects an unplaceable Europeanese accent to induce people to underestimate his intelligence.)

Mr. Flynn. Welcome.

FLYNN

Please you, call of me Randy.

VICTORIA

As in Rhandy-manthus?

FLYNN

Haw haw haw. Randy is fine.

VICTORIA
(With a flourish)

Randy, what do you consider your . . . grrrreatest inspiration?

FLYNN

Well, not many known, but once in time for stories, I wanted for myself an actor to be. To rule all-a-world from the stage, haw haw, I thought and ambitioned.

VICTORIA

Although apparently it can be done. One of the most powerful men in the world today is a former actor. What do you think about the American president, Randy?

FLYNN
(As if from a script)

I agree most heartedly with current stance that national government takes on

rhadamanthus

Mr. Reagan. I feel, this for present, no doubt the most responsible position for Sporqish welfare and reputation, and most according to Sporqish character.

VICTORIA

(Somber)

I couldn't agree more.

FLYNN

(Brightly)

But I'm gladdening you intone America, because for my own career was motivated of spectacular events by that country history, so characteristic of that country.

VICTORIA

(Tone impossible to read)

Oh, I don't doubt it. Americans are always so totally in their character, whatever they do.

FLYNN

I challenge all other-ones to say anywise! So. In late of nineteenth century was an American famous outlaw benamed Jesse James, who robbing of banks and trains and sometimes kill people.

VICTORIA

Sounds like quite a rogue!

FLYNN

But much cunningly and yearsomely he evaded captures. Meanwhile, with help from newspapers, he portrayed that alike Robin Hood, he just robbing richies to pay poories, but *also* very murdersome, and *also* completely innocent. Also, as I say, he is never caught. For this, was very much hero of his own daytime.

VICTORIA

I like him already!

FLYNN

But although much-loved, the people very afraid to get shoot or stealed by this herosome man. So the governments place on him a bounty. Eventually one of his own gang betrays. This ganger, a Mr. Robert Ford, shoots Mr. Jane and kills him. Boon!
    (Mimes gun)

VICTORIA
    (With unclear connotation)

What an American!

FLYNN

Shoots in the back of the head while Mr. James dusting a picture. With a big feather.
    (Miming)
Broosh broosh broosh.

VICTORIA

My my.

FLYNN

The American government does not imprison or put to dead this Mr. Ford for the murder. Okay. Mr. Jame was a most wanted man. But here is for surprise.
    (Leaning toward VICTORIA as if sharing a secret,
    but addressing the camera)
For years after, this Mr. Ford performs *in a play*, playing himself, about how he shooted a de-armed man—and no any man, the great American heroist and his friend!—in the head of the back while he feather dusts a paint picture. Notice that: details all the same! The feather: here; the dusty: here; the picture—

actually, interesting this: of all things, he change the picture! I think was of a horse. Must have been not nice horse!

                        VICTORIA

"I cannot tell a lie." Wasn't that what the American president said?

                        FLYNN

Characteristical Americanism. I can only telling lies about my taste in the art, yes?

                        VICTORIA

Haw haw.

                        FLYNN
                (Slapping the back of his head)

Anyway, back of the back, boon! This play, Mr. Ford performs hundreds, almost a thousand times. About how he shooted this most dangerous man while he do housework.

                        VICTORIA
                (Mugging the camera)

Hire a maid, I always say!

                        FLYNN

Sometimes the audience shout, "Huzzah to you, Mr. Ford. Brains on the walls, how *très chic* home decor. Like Marla Stewart with a pistolet, you!" Other times, "Hallo, Mr. Ford. Show the famous cowardice now! Picking a fight with the back turned, feathers up! Maybe think you hunting peacock, non?"

                        VICTORIA
                (Obviously confused)

Americans love hunting. Davy Crockett.

FLYNN

The play was called, without much imagining, How I Shoot Jesse Jane. Parentheses, I am guessing, Into the Head-Back While Dusting.

VICTORIA

Haw haw.

FLYNN

This play the childbrain of a theaterman whom I admire greatly. He geniused to take this Ford and make him repeat on stage, again and again and again. The shootment. Not only theater this, no. Alchemy. Because what is a Ford? A living, breath-making personage, yes? with dreams, fears, hurts—okay! Now, in view of the everybody, he am changed down, performance by performance, to the one action. Over and over, you see? Until not just in public imagining does he become only this, The Man Who Shooted Jesse Jame, but in his own mind.

VICTORIA
(Nodding like a robot)
Repetition is extremely transformative.

FLYNN

Some thinks it can make believe of non-believers.

VICTORIA
(Still reading from the prompter)
I've been asking the exact same questions in these interviews for eighteen years now. "Mr. or Ms. So-and-such, what do you consider your . . . grrrreatest inspiration?"

FLYNN

Whatever you are, the repetition makes you. It becomes, how you say, inscribed in the muscular!

rhadamanthus

VICTORIA

I haven't varied the intonation of that question in over a decade. For the first hundred shows, I tried to say it a little different each time, but eventually I realized there wasn't any point.

FLYNN

Unthinking, a reflex.

VICTORIA

(Ignoring the prompter)

I no longer know what "inspiration" even means. I'm sure I used to know. When people come up to me in the street, they say, "Victoria, you've always been *my* inspiration." They don't seem to know what it means either. I've permanently obliterated the meaning of this word for both myself and thousands of viewers. The worst part is, I haven't the faintest idea if this is good, or bad, or what.

FLYNN

Absolutely, Victoria, you obtain it exactly. Now you are inspiring me!

VICTORIA

(Blushing)

Why thank you, Randy! I accept the compliment.

FLYNN

For more extreme happenings, such as shooteding your friend, the repetition is built in. The person relives in the head many, many times—even when no people watch. Picture inside the Ford: Sometimes it happens the same, he shoots—just as in the realism, okay. But sometimes, for fantasy, the Ford allows himself other option: he step away from the history. He says, "No, this time I do not shoot." Maybe instead he say, "Okay, Jess Jame, because we are such friends, let us go bank-rob today, just like in olden weeks." You see?

Because, the Ford says, "I do not want always to be the shooter. I break from the shooting I have done." Because otherwise the burden is unbearable.

(An awkward pause.)

VICTORIA
(Hushed, conspiratorially)
Sometimes when I'm on a bender, I like to ask the shot glass what inspires it to hold so much whiskey.

FLYNN
(Undistracted)
Now put Ford upon a stage. Write in big letters on the marquee, How I Shot the Jame, yes? Now the Ford replays not in his mind but
   (Pauses, gestures dramatically)
in front of the audience. Can he choosing not to shoot here? People have give moneys to him shooting. When the Jess makes for to dusting—"Here I go," he says, "off to showing the back to you"—the Ford does not turn to the audience and say, "You know what? Tonight I do not shoot." No. Why? Because, no sense. The audience will say to the Ford, "Look here, I paid the moneys, now I will see the shooting." So the Ford will shoot. Yes, because he wants moneys, but mostly because—because why not? Mr. Jones is already dead. The Ford not shooting today will not bring him back, will not unshoot the Jess. The Ford thinks no harm can come from shooting again.
   (Slaps his armrest)
Wrong. Each time the Ford shoots, he becomes more the Shooter, less the Mr. Ford. Narrower and narrower and narrower, until exists only at one point: 3 April, 1882, between 8 and 9 am, St. Joseph, Missouri, USA. All other Ford is poof! Gone.

VICTORIA
You can always tell a performer who gives 110 percent.

rhadamanthus

FLYNN

In the Middle Ages, they say hell is place where you burn in fire, where they pour stickum-hot lead in the mouth hole so you cannot even scream. Rhadamanthus—this is me in the *Spoofhole*, according—Rhadamanthus says no. Hell is a stage for you to commit your sin over and over. In life, you stab once? Okay. In hell you stab hundred thousand times. In life you seduce best friend's wife? In hell you seduce in front

(Gestures)

so everybody watched. In hell, crime is the punishment. And—here where I appear—in Dodoville, crime will also be

(Smiles and turns toward the camera)

the entertainment. And Mountebank Theater to be the place: come on down for a reasonable price.

VICTORIA

(Apparently in earnest)

So your next production will be The Shooting of Jesse James.

FLYNN

(Nonplussed)

Metaphorically, yes. What I do at the Mountebank is filling my stage with Fords. You commit a crime in Dodoville, okay. Laws do not prosecute, okay. Maybe you have a big friend, he help you twist arms or pay off the moneys. Fine, Randy will offer you *more money*. He will give an audience. They will come in evening dress, and you perform your the shooting for them again. Or perhaps you did not shoot: you steal the orphanage, you throw big baseball game, you drown the bitchy wife, whatever. Randy pay you do it again at the Mountebank. Big musical numbers on stage with you, showgirls with feathers—not for dusting, haw haw haw—jugglers, fire-eaters. Because Dodoville *loves* its Fords, *loves* its musical numbers, *loves* big productions.

VICTORIA

Oh, it's true, Randy. I do love it all, the singing, the dancing, the big sets, the costumes. I hope I don't get in trouble for saying this, but I'd watch those girls mop the floor if the costume was fancy enough.

FLYNN

Haw, haw, maybe that I try! No, for kid: the girls do not understand mop. But as I talking before: in America, for How I Am Shoot, sometimes audience cheer the Ford, sometimes boo. In Dodoville, the characteristic is: hero, coward, we don't care, we just want the shootment. Over and over and over, we love it! Oh, maybe a sourcat hiss, "Grr, that Ford, I am so ill of him, let he shoot somebody new!" But in really what he want is new musical number, new juggling, new fire-eating. Okay, so Randy Flynn, this he will provide. But same ol' shooting, always always always. This I promise.
   (Smiles at camera and winks)

VICTORIA

Well, you heard it here folks. Come on out to the Mountebank Theater, where somebody always get shot.
   (Her grin grows wide and uncomfortable)
And come see me, Victoria Schmutz, on Tuesday and Thursday nights for my new one-woman show, *How I Replaced Ginger Adams as Host of Inspiring People*.
   (Screen displays promotional poster. VICTORIA
   SCHMUTZ smeared with war paint and biting older
   well-coiffed woman in the back of the neck)
Until next week: stay inspired!

   (DAGGETT turns off the video player and exits.)

            (BLACKOUT)

SCENE three

(SETTING: Ten months in the past. RANDALL FLYNN's office.)

(ON RISE: RANDALL FLYNN walks SERGIO PACK from the door to his desk.)

FLYNN
Come in, come in! Are you ready for your first leading role? I've cast you as Hamlet, Pack.

SERGIO
Oh boy! I can't wait to sink my teeth into something fresh.

FLYNN
We'll stage the play in our own time and place: Dodoville, the Aluminum City, 1986.

SERGIO

I can do the accent, at least.

FLYNN

About a decade ago, a new generation inherited our city's chief industry. Men like Samson Loogey, who forsook their fathers' scrupulous business practices. Instead, their underhanded dealings and narcissistic posturing helped drag our nation into war with our neighbors. We'll use Samson as a model for your Hamlet.

SERGIO

Brilliant! That guy always looks great in a suit.

FLYNN

We lost the war and now bear the humiliating yoke of foreign occupation. All because these lordlings pressed their personal advantage at the expense of the rest of us.

SERGIO

"Find the opportunity in every disaster." My mom says that's the hallmark of greatness.

FLYNN
(Nodding, quietly impressed by SERGIO's stupidity)

As I said, we'll fashion your Hamlet after Samson's ilk: self-centered, ambitious, yet reckless. Above all, with an unshakable sense of entitlement. Do you think you can play that?

SERGIO

Damn well earned the chance, at any rate!

rhadamanthus

FLYNN

We'll dress you in Samson's distinct style: stovepipe rebelliously half-cocked and fob chain a-dangle. You will embody the greed, the laziness, the duplicity of men like him. Something is rotten in the city of Dodoville. In a word, its Hamlets.

SERGIO

Fantastic. Also, there's monologues, right? I prefer them, actually.

FLYNN

To drive our message home, we'll emphasize his relationship with Polonius. We've cast Bobby Cashmere. Do you know him, Pack? The most lovable Polonius anyone will ever see. Ours will be the tragedy of a saintly old gentleman whom Prince Hamlet kills carelessly, callously, with no repentance.

SERGIO

Polonius? I don't remember him as such a saint.

FLYNN

And sagely.

SERGIO

(Confused)

He's an idiot.

FLYNN

Directors have staged it that way because they rubber stamp Hamlet's estimation of him, and Hamlet treats him with contempt.

SERGIO

. . . Because Polonius is contemptuous?

FLYNN
(Sourly)

These are British productions, American productions. From countries whose concept of power is industrial and military might. Here in Dodoville, however, we appreciate, shall we say, other forms of influence.

SERGIO

The greasy kind.

FLYNN

Grease. We, like Polonius, know how to get by—and even prosper—without the traditional advantages. To be the winners whom history forgets. So that our culture—our very souls—are not poisoned by the corruptive rot of empire. Its ownership.

SERGIO

I dunno, I think Polonius comes off pretty bad.

FLYNN

As the king's chamberlain, Polonius recognizes the first rule of Dodovillean survival: to appear exactly as he's expected. To *seem*, not to be. "Being" is a luxury most people cannot afford, especially in the workplace.

SERGIO

Are you calling Hamlet luxuriant, then? As a "be"-er.

FLYNN

Indulging in luxuries, yes. Hamlet assumes Polonius must be buffoonish, or calculating, or both. In fact, an egoist like Hamlet expects foolishness from everyone who does not agree he ought to be in charge. Very well. Polonius simply, wisely, obliges expectation. He *seems*. Just as until recent years, we Dodovilleans maintained our autonomy by seeming too unteachably simple to comprehend the Cold War ideologies of either Superpower. Because what would anyone expect from a people foolish enough to build their city at the base of an active volcano?

                          SERGIO
Mm. Polonius may actually be a buffoon.

                          FLYNN
Why? Because his advice is an encyclopedia of empty platitudes. Or is it? "Neither a borrower nor a lender be." Behold, our economy undone by bad loans. "Beware entrance to a quarrel, but being in it, make thy opponent beware you." Two lessons our conduct in the last war will readily affirm. Or no? Dodovilleans do not mistake common wisdom for banality—only arrogance does that. Here in Dodoville, Polonius represents the accumulated knowledge and cunning of generations. And our Hamlet spits on him. Literally spits. Ptuh! Right in the eye.

                          SERGIO
I don't want to spit on anybody.

                          FLYNN
Acting. Just make the sound. Ptuh! Try it with me.

                          SERGIO
P-tuh.

                          FLYNN
Work on it. This abuse builds and builds—until Hamlet murders the charming old man without any rhyme or reason.

                          SERGIO
Hm? Polonius was in hiding, and Hamlet mistook him for the king, his father's killer.

FLYNN

Impossible. Why would a king hide in his own palace? And from Hamlet, that insignificant shit? The voice behind the arras called out for help. Couldn't Hamlet tell it wasn't the king? Not just any man, his uncle the king! Three times it called out. Help, help, help!

SERGIO

I know what three is.

FLYNN

So. The beloved vessel of traditional wisdom senselessly slain by a spoiled, rash young man. That's our angle.

SERGIO

Rash? That's the first I've heard Hamlet called that. Usually the opposite.

FLYNN

Read the text. He constantly surrenders to whims, he has almost no self-control. Says whatever comes into his head—mean, vicious things. Stabs the first thing that moves. All without a twinge of conscience.

SERGIO

But . . . he's unable to resolve himself to slay the king and avenge his father.

FLYNN

Because he doesn't want to! Think: because what must follow? Either he's punished for regicide or he becomes king himself. Both serious constraints on his freedom, and he's not so serious a man! He'd much rather sulk, be a burden to the state and an embarrassment to everybody—just like the traitors to our city, who have hoarded wealth and prestige but refuse to take up the responsibility of governance. Who have carelessly trod on the Poloniuses whom they consider worthless. Politically or otherwise.

rhadamanthus

SERGIO

Well, perhaps they—

FLYNN

And that will be our point: today's Dodoville reaps the consequence of moral indifference. On account of Hamletizing, our entire state has been upended, left open to foreign domination. Americans who won't let us rebuild a post office without permission.

SERGIO

Okay, yes. A bit like home, I suppose.

FLYNN

The murder of Polonius. The entire tragedy of the play flows forth from this one—I repeat, rash—action. All the carnage that transpires, all the public and private reversals of fortune, stem from this death at the center of the play. And the greatest casualty: Denmark.

SERGIO

Or Dodoville, the other "D." Is that the conceit?

FLYNN

The trick was how to stage it here in town. The text itself offered the clue. Lobby. Hamlet hides Polonius' body in the lobby of Elsinore Castle. Do castles have lobbies?

SERGIO

(Getting it)

Hotels do.

FLYNN

We'll create the Denmark Hotel right here in Dodoville. A perfect complement to the Norway, byword for local luxury. We'll reproduce the

will madden

Norway's iconic lobby as the Denmark: the marble floor, red velvet walls, the crystal chandelier. Ceiling-high mirrors, because Hamlet will be nothing if not vain. The grand staircase—and of course, the lavish fountain filled with exotic fishes.

SERGIO
(Uncertain)
I like it. But can you carry the Polonius conceit through to the end? As you said, he dies about halfway through, and you nearly forget him by the final curtain.

FLYNN
(Visibly excited)
Ah. In our version, the show stopper will come in Act IV. We'll do a big reveal for the discovery of Polonius slain. Shakespeare has it off-stage but we'll place it on—plan the entire production around it. Court attendants open the hatch under the stairs and the old man's rancid body falls out. Not just a dummy stirring up some dust. I've arranged for insects—automatons, wait till you see—they explode from the carcass and scatter toward the wings. The stage crew rigged up a test for me this morning. Let me tell you, Pack, people will be talking about this for years. Chittering: mlep mlep mlep. You can really hear it coming from these things.

SERGIO
They won't get on me, will they?

FLYNN
Maybe we'll put Ophelia on stage too. Creepy-crawlies grown fat on her father's flesh scurry up her limbs. Her dress. They bite her, try to . . .
(Covers himself with a hand)
In our production, no one wonders why she kills herself later.

rhadamanthus

SERGIO

Ew.

FLYNN

This spectacle will be the linchpin of the whole shebang. The audience will be stunned by the visceral horror.

SERGIO

Good. I like when theater makes people feel things.

FLYNN

For the rest of the play, we never let the power of that moment dissipate. On the king's orders, Polonius' vestments are hung over the stage, with a hole over the heart where Hamlet's sword ran him through. Shot him. It's the twentieth century, let's have Hamlet shoot Polonius. Huge hole, as if a cannonball. Golden light shines out from behind. Piercing. The audience will almost have to shield its eyes. A remembrance of what's been done. It says: This is what happens. This is what happens when you give rein to the cowardice and savagery of a spoiled prince.

SERGIO

But is that enough to—

FLYNN

Then the big finale. Corpses heaped in a pile: Claudius the king, Gertrude the queen, Hamlet, Laertes. The blood spreads across the stage. Fortinbras slumps off early, to keep his booties dry. Horatio follows, before he can open his yap. Shut up, Horatio! Leaving us alone to survey the carnage. All dead. But wait! Polonius' garment falls from the ceiling and lands atop the king. Is . . . did I just see it move? The king, he's lying there in his own blood, but he's still alive. The living, the dying embodiment of Denmark—of Dodoville!—moves. He tries to sit up, to disentangle himself from the dead man's cloak, but he can't. And

. . . and he speaks. Faintly, weakly, not even audible at first, you only think you hear. But gradually it becomes louder, more insistent. Just a single word over and over. H-h-help. Help. Again. Help. Over and over. Little chirps, like a baby bird. Help. Hellllp. Slowly the curtain falls. Shh, shh. The house lights stay down. We're in the dark. For minutes, that's all there is: help, help. Claudius can barely form the word, you have to strain. H-h-help. Oh, how long will this go on? Till it's totally obscene! Even the audience wonders if they oughtn't get up and aid this poor, dying man who calls pathetically for help. Well, shouldn't they?! Then it stops. We wait. Nothing. O gods, nothing! Then Hamlet's voice—your voice, Pack!—repeats his final line. "And the rest is silence."

SERGIO
(Chilled)
Chilling.

FLYNN
Yes? O Toledo! It'll kill 'em, surefire. So, Pack, you in? I won't do it with anybody but you. It's you or nobody, the whole thing's off. Here, I've taken the liberty of preparing the papers.

SERGIO
(Signing the documents)
Pen won't work.

FLYNN
(Handing him another)
Our Hamlet is the worst possible person, believing himself deserving to rule on account of his birth, yet holding himself too sacrosanct to be sullied by state governance. As consequence, he leaves behind a swath of ruin entirely out of proportion to his importance. Socially relevant today. And! It'll provide the boost your career needs so badly.

rhadamanthus

SERGIO

(Shaking pen)

This one neither.

FLYNN

You'll be participating in something historical here. We won't just make Dodoville Shakespearean. We'll make Shakespeare Dodovillean.

(BLACKOUT)

SCENE four

(SETTING: 1976, nine years previous. A crowded tavern called The Skinned Rhino on Richelieu Avenue. Patrons are vivacious black-and-white cardboard cutouts.)

(AT RISE: SERGIO PACK, 19, sits at the bar. He wears a bright-colored dress shirt, collar unbuttoned, with sleeves rolled to the elbow. Suffering from the summer heat, he draws a perspiring beer bottle across his forehead. RANDALL FLYNN enters dressed in his scarlet doorman liveries. The temperature does not seem to affect him. He sits on the stool next to SERGIO, placing his large bell on the counter. The BARTENDER smiles and brings him his usual, a pint of water with one ice cube. The conversation with SERGIO begins in dumbshow. FLYNN introduces himself and orders SERGIO a water too. SERGIO pushes it away and drains his beer. He does not want to talk. FLYNN shrugs and leaves him be. Now SERGIO begins to monologue. Alternately, he pounds his fist and appeals for sympathy. FLYNN's posture denotes sincere attention. Suddenly, SERGIO slams his glass down and asks with an overlarge gesture, So what do you do? FLYNN indicates first his livery, then the bell, before explaining his Sunday afternoon ritual. SERGIO slaps the bar and interrupts.)

SERGIO

(Slurring slightly)

Fascinating because, you can probably tell by my carriage, I am an actor. From early on, acting had the utmost importance for me. To act or not to act: when *that* became the question, I decided I'd have my answer. Namely, to act. Whatever the impulse, just act. For always 'tis nobler to. To.

FLYNN

May I ask what inspired this . . . this decision?

SERGIO

Just my nature.
    (A beat)
Maybe one thing. But it's painful, I never talk about it.

FLYNN

If you think that's best.

SERGIO

I was thirteen or so. My parents were in Zahzia for a botany symposium. Oh, I was fiercely independent at that age! Cunning, tenacious. Like those Remorse District brats, but cleaner. Nevertheless, I was entrusted to the care of my grandfather. Not to watch me of course, no. Strictly in case of emergency. But even though I didn't need supervision, I permitted him to make me lunch. For the sake of polity, let's call it.

FLYNN

... Sure.

SERGIO

When I'd still been a child, Grandad and I had been fond playmates. Swing sets, plush orangutans, model trains. Whatever puerility amused him. But now as my intellect branched out, I realized I could no longer permit my intellectual growth to be impeded by my grandfather's facile entertainments. It was imperative I withdraw from his company in order to pursue more sophistifying activity. So after lunch, I went up to the attic alone to play with my toys.

(A beat)

Maybe an hour later, I heard a loud crash downstairs.

(A long pause, as SERGIO seems to forget his story entirely. FLYNN touches his sleeve.)

In the library, my parents kept towering stacks arboreal catalogs, tall as, well, trees. One of them could easily have teetered and fell. My mother, too, used to paint portraits on life-sized dominoes—these fell over all the time. Basically, our house was a wonderland of things that might collapse and clatter. Nevertheless, I felt certain the sound I'd just heard had one and only one possible cause: Grandad falling down the cellar stairs.

(SERGIO stares into his glass while FLYNN waits.)

rhadamanthus

I had never heard a crash quite like this before, but I had determined, by means of my pers . . . perspicat—

FLYNN

Perspicacity.

SERGIO

—that it had been the sound of a body, a mammalian body, a mammal of certain size which precluded all but my grandfather's body, and which was in no way a duck.

FLYNN

(Smiling faintly)
Certainly not a plush orangutan.

SERGIO

No. Furthermore, I could tell Grandad had not collapsed on the parlor floor, having nodded off and fallen out of his chair. I had determined, via the acuity of my perspir . . .

FLYNN

Just say perceptiveness.

SERGIO

—that he had fallen down some stairs. Moreover, it had not been the steps between the front parlor and the rest of the house. I could tell on account of the vector and mm . . .

FLYNN

(Trying to be helpful)
Direction. Degree and quality of muffledness.

SERGIO

Precisely! Also, it had not been the stairs between the first and second floors, nor the stairs between the second floor and the attic, but the cellar stairs. From the first floor down to the cellar. Nor, as I said previously, had Grandad dropped, say, a box of hammers. No, he had fallen down it bodily.

FLYNN

Body and all. Not a duck.

SERGIO

In summation, I had heard a crash upon the stairs, the stairs to the cellar, which had been caused by the rapid precipitation of a body, my grandfather's body. I had discerned all these things, with certainty, from the sound alone.

FLYNN

(Choosing to be impressed)

Impressive.

SERGIO

Wait, what you don't know! On account of my parents having just attained a new plateau of professional success, being the first ever to achieve spectacular wealth in the natural sciences—

FLYNN

Oh, you're one of the Packs? The botanists? Did your family really make all that money in research? I've always wondered if there wasn't some sort of hanky-panky going on.

SERGIO

(Visibly insulted)

Understandable mistake, but no. It's simply a fact that my parents so revolutionarily advanced the global store of floral, arboreal, shrubular, and grassant knowledge that exorbitant financial recompense became the inevitable result.

FLYNN

Makes sense.

SERGIO

In any case, we had just purchased a new home. This was not the house I had grown up in, whose every clank and creak I'd memorized since I was old enough to toddle. This was a new house, a Takoberu design. They are always full of secret entrances and exits, some of which I was still discovering. For instance, I had just learned that waterfowl could reach the artificial grotto beneath the house—

FLYNN

Oh, I see. There's the ducks.

SERGIO

—by swimming through a flooded channel fed by the pond outside. Of course they didn't though. Swim it, I mean.

FLYNN

So, there were no ducks.

SERGIO

But there could be! The point is, in such environment, my inference had been extraordinary.

FLYNN

De-duck-tion.

SERGIO

Correct. But here's the thing: having ascertained the cause of the sound, I did nothing.

(FLYNN orders SERGIO another water. He drinks one gulp, frowns, and pushes it away.)

You might not be able to guess, since I'm so well-adjusted now, but as a child I was prone to fits of rage. To the point I'd refuse to speak to people—complete incommunicados for offenses slight, imagined, or both. Funny thing is, I don't recall having been angry at Grandad—even though he'd been extremely strict for a grandparent. Inverse to the usual pattern: having indulged my mother to the utmost degree, he now seemed to regret it. Whenever they had an argument, he'd rumble at her, "Oh, and I let you get away with murder!" That would put an end to *that* discussion, let me tell you.

FLYNN

(Making a note)

Interesting.

SERGIO

But me on the other hand, if I ever got caught burning down the house of, say, the chairwoman of some academic committee, whoa boy, I'd get in soooo much trouble with Grandad. It'd hardly even matter that she wasn't supposed to be at home at the time! On account of the principle, you know?

(Wipes sweat off his brow)

But even though he was strict with me, I was never particularly fearful of him. Nor had I become so engrossed in my playing. My parents believed in educational toys. I had all these Mendel-inspired games. Pollination Crossfire. Increase the Wheat, did you ever play that one? Graft It Like You Mean It, A Nightmare on Dutch Elm Street, Pistils A'Blazin'.

rhadamanthus

FLYNN

Wonderful!

SERGIO

None of them are as fun as they sound. Point is, I'd been so bored at the time, I might have jumped at the opportunity to do anything else. But I didn't check if Grandad had fallen. To this day, I have no idea why.

FLYNN

Perhaps you were afraid of what you would find.

SERGIO

(Considers)

I don't think so, no. If the fall was bad, I could alert the physician we kept on call. Perhaps I was just afraid to find out I'd been wrong. Because—and I think this is significant—this was the first time I'd had such a specific intuition. Part of growing up is you learn how to trust your instincts, you start knowing things without quite knowing how you know them. This had never really happened to me before. The rumble and crash I'd heard had so many potential causes, but Grandad falling down the cellar stairs had been my first and only thought. The more I replayed the sound in my head, the more certain I felt this was the only interpretation. What a powerful feeling! I guess I was afraid to lose that?

(SERGIO waits for a response. FLYNN appears about to give one but doesn't.)

Or, what may have happened: I was overcome by my sense of powerlessness at seeing my grandfather age, who, let me assure you, had never been so old in the past. Once he had been hale and hearty—up on ladders and down on his knees out in the garden. He led an active lifestyle, is what people would say. But chores he once cheerfully offered to do, he no longer did. As result of this decline, he now was lying in a heap at the bottom of the cellar stairs. I probably didn't want to face how *un*-hearty he'd become. In-hale, whatever.

(Clearly suffering from the heat, SERGIO orders a whiskey) Instead of investigating, I listened for sounds that would contradict my intuition, some sign Grandad was not at the bottom of the stairs: him picking up books which had fallen over in the library, for instance. But I heard nothing. Which wasn't strange. Those days, Grandad spent much of the afternoon napping in his chair. Perhaps he had slept through the crash. I realized what I might expect to hear was the same whether Grandad had fallen or not. I continued to play in the attic.

(Sucks whiskey from an ice cube, then presses it to his neck) I couldn't even concentrate on hating my toys. The idea of Grandad broken at the bottom of the stairs distracted me. But by now, so much time had passed, I was actually afraid to investigate. To get caught investigating, I mean. Because if I had heard it before, why did I come running only now?

FLYNN

(With compassion)

We feel legitimate in the heat of the moment. But later, we think if we meant to do it, we would have done it already.

SERGIO

I found myself trying to invent an excuse for checking the cellar. Harder than you might imagine. I paced the attic floor pondering this problem, in hope my pacing would awaken my grandfather and induce him to investigate me. Whereas, what needed was for me to go down to investigate him. Before I went, I spent forty-five minutes inventing a reason.

FLYNN

Which was?

SERGIO

Mom and Dad frowned upon me going down there alone. On account of the grotto. They now considered it an irresponsible thing for parents to have in the basement: a child could drown, wild ducks and geese might peck him to death! Well, I decided I was old enough to get attacked by a goddamned duck if I wanted to.

       (SERGIO waits for FLYNN to nod in agreement. He doesn't.)

I found Grandad splayed at the bottom of the stairs. His face was red 'cause his head was downward. His legs were bent around his body in an ugly way.

       FLYNN

What was the experience like?

       SERGIO

My initial reaction, funny as this sounds, I was surprised to find him there. All this time knowing he was there, when I got there, I didn't expect to see him.

       FLYNN
       (With a touch of indulgence)

Hmm. There's a kind of disconnect between deduction and reality. We experience a tiny sense of miracle every time the math works.

       SERGIO

Standing atop the stairs and seeing him there, it felt like a dream had invaded the real world. I wanted to take a picture, to convince myself later it'd really happened.

       FLYNN

And then?

       SERGIO

"Sergionus!" I heard. My grandfather's voice. He was trying to hold out his hand to me. "Sergionus, I called to you, but you didn't come. I called for help. Like this: Help. Help me. Help. Please help. Oh help me. Help. I need help. Oh, Sergionus, I kept calling. For help. But you didn't come." "But Grandad," I said, "I didn't hear you call!" Which was true. But the fall I *had* heard. Although it sounded like it could've been anything! Only now did I realize it couldn't have been anything else.

FLYNN
You realize you've been telling me exactly the opposite?

SERGIO
Both versions are true, somehow.

FLYNN
I see.

SERGIO
Oh, my poor grandfather, I thought, falling stair by stair. Striking, breaking, contorting. It's something I've never really forgiven myself for. Not because he died after. I mean, the paramedic said heart attack. In scenarios like these, medical attention, an hour one way or the other, it never matters. But what I can never get past is, why I had felt so paralyzed when helping would have taken so little effort and my help might have made all the difference?

(FLYNN's and SERGIO's eyes lock in an understanding glance. Finally, SERGIO turns away and looks back to his drink.)

FLYNN
Well, Mr. Pack. Perhaps one day you and I will make a study of it.

(CURTAIN)

ACT three
SCENE one

(SETTING: 1979, three years later. Party at the Norway Hotel to celebrate the ascension of SAMSON LOOGEY to ganglord after the passing of his father, Chancel.)

(AT RISE: Revelers in fancy dress, wearing hats of aluminum foil in stylish designs. Among them, director VIKTOR PLINKO with a stained shirt.)

(Enter two GOONS, tipsy. Both are lowbrow with affected speech.)

                    GOON 1

So Chancel Loogey's finally sawed off.

GOON 2

I never loved the twisted ol' oak, but I'll say this: under him everybody knew what was expected, and everybody knew what happened when what's expected didn't, so everything budded beautiful. I'm sorry to have him gone.

GOON 1

Surprised to see the aluminum business handed over to the son, Samson.

GOON 2

Whom else would it go? Old man only had the one son.

GOON 1

But he didn't trust him! Chancel was a sort to keep his secrets mucked, so when Samson free-flashed the family hand, he'd lose the father's confidence. And also.

GOON 2

What?

GOON 1

Well, the rumor's going round. You know that kook in Krompachy, the one who rings the bell and hollers at tourists?

GOON 2

Name 'a Flynn, I think. Rhadalmalthus.

GOON 1

They say he's another Loogey sprout.

GOON 2

(Taken aback)

Forget it, the two look nothing alike! Plus, I thought Flynn was a foreigner, what with that incipherable manner of yap.

rhadamanthus

GOON 1

Young men sometimes sow their barley abroad—that's a thing you might've heard! They say when Flynn's mother found out Loogey was a money tree in this country, she moved to Dodoville to see if she couldn't graft herself to his fortune. But he turned her away with pockets full of mulch.

GOON 2

(Quietly)

Loogey Sr. bought into aluminum with the wife's money. Can't blame him for keeping his weeds whacked.

GOON 1

But when the wife got clipped a year ago, it's known Chancel rewrote his will and testament. Maybe Flynn thought it might've kept better faith to all Chancel's offshoots, especially with papa so luke on Samson, but. Story short, didn't happen.

GOON 2

No. Interesting, though, that Flynn always maligned the Loogeys with more than his regular brimstone.

GOON 1

And that's why, I'd say. Flynn grew up in poverty, wanting revenge on account of his denied paternity.

GOON 2

Well, nuts to him. Samson is ganglord now.

GOON 1

The son hasn't half the patience the father had.
(Whispering)
Likely his downfall. Aluminum's on rusty roots, needing cultivation by a sage hand. Meanwhile, the Department grows stronger every day.

(Displays a secret hand signal)

GOON 2

(Offers the countersign, then speaks loud enough for others to hear)

Samson's a man who makes short, bloody work of his enemies. Only a fool would cross him!

GOON 1

I'll cross him for a favor yet—I've a bushel of debts I need pruned off. Plus, if I'm lucky, it's a favor Samson won't have time to claim return on.

GOON 2

Careful. Time's enough you'll wear a black ring for that.

GOON 1

A black ring means I've still got the fingers to wear one. Pardon me, I'll take my chances. Your introduction for my round, how 'bout it?

GOON 2

(Shaking hands)

That's change! Follow me.

(GOONS exit.)

(Enter SERGIO PACK with PHILIP HUMPHREY. SERGIO still wears his younger man's clothes. HUMPHREY is without glasses, carrying a tragedian's mask and wearing buskins.)

SERGIO

Humphrey! You've got to introduce me to Viktor Plinko. The director who's launched a thousand careers!

rhadamanthus

HUMPHREY

Not mine. My star's on the decline these days. Must've been my sister getting me all my work before, 'cause today I can't even wait tables in this town.

SERGIO

Well, Plinko knows you, doesn't he?

HUMPHREY

He's familiar with my cakehole, but it no longer pleases him to feed it.

SERGIO

That's a start enough for me. Point him out.

HUMPHREY

Fine, that's him over there.
    (Points to PLINKO)

SERGIO

The one with the melon stain on his shirt?

HUMPHREY

How do you know it's melon?

SERGIO

    (Crestfallen)
'Cause it's melon punch I spilled on him not ten minutes ago.

HUMPHREY

Ay! Well, the news for you is, he's been slipped onto Loogey's finger. Became a vassal to keep his theater open. Means he might give you some lines if he likes you, but plum parts go for doing the Loogeys favors.

SERGIO

(Tentatively)

What sort of favor does Loogey require?

HUMPHREY

Don't think of it. The dirty kind. Strong-arming and intimidation for light stuff. Just suck up your pride. Look, the stain's near laughed off his shirt already. Come, we'll talk to him.

(Enter SAMSON LOOGEY, his outfit the obvious inspiration for SERGIO's future Hamlet. With LOUISTENANT on his left.)

SERGIO

(Studying LOOGEY)

Perhaps my career needs to blaze a trail into more daring environs. To the bold go the spoils!

HUMPHREY

(Surprised)

You are not intimidating.

SERGIO

I could *act* intimidating. Carriage, that's all it is. I've practiced intimidating characters in my bedroom mirror.

HUMPHREY

(Holding SERGIO back)

You'll find Samson Loogey a less forgiving audience.

SERGIO

(Shaking him off)

Still, no better school for art than experience.

rhadamanthus

HUMPHREY

But don't start here. Maybe your parents could get you something in academia. Blackjack work.

SERGIO

Mother says I haven't got the grit for the academy. She suggested I try the mob.

HUMPHREY

Have no illusions. Aluminum is a killing field, Sergio.

SERGIO

And don't be surprised if I have the mettle. Remember: some of the deadlier poisons are botanical.
   (SERGIO assumes a thuggish posture. HUMPHREY,
    who would might have otherwise laughed, looks despaired.)
Wish me luck.

HUMPHREY

Long life or a quick death!
   (Softly)
Not likely either.
   (Exits.)

   (SERGIO approaches LOOGEY)

SERGIO

Hello, Samson. Congratulations on your ascension.

LOOGEY

You are?

SERGIO

   (Cracking his knuckles)
Forrest Wallops.

LOOGEY

(Turning away)

I don't know who that is.

SERGIO

Perhaps that's an asset. I'm told you are the sort of man who sometimes needs unpleasant business taken care of. And I might be the man to do it.

LOOGEY

I don't know what unpleasant business you mean. Perhaps you're looking to clean toilets. Are you a janitor, Mr. Wallops?

SERGIO

You might say that. Except the filth I clean up is the human kind. People who have misplaced the money they owe you, or the respect due to you, or the secret they were supposed to keep for you. Or maybe they're just thinking of misplacing it. I clean that mess up and stow it in the proper receptacle.

LOOGEY

You ever perform this kind of work before? You have a resume, Mr. Wallops?

SERGIO

(Defiant)

I'm sorry, I've forgotten the names of my previous employers.

LOOGEY

I don't know what you've heard, but my business is aluminum, not custodial services.

SERGIO

I've never heard otherwise. But should the need arise.

rhadamanthus

LOOGEY

And should it arise, what were you expecting in way of compensation?

SERGIO
(Menacing)

For a man like me, sometimes the pleasure of the work is payment enough.

LOOGEY
(Sourly)

On occasion when it's not, though?

SERGIO

I've a friend, an actor, his name is Sergio Pack. Some day he might like a role in a Viktor Plinko production. I heard in your spare time you help out his casting director.

LOOGEY

I tell you what. You want a job, go up to room 313 tomorrow night. You can meet with one of my custodial managers. We're fully staffed, but this is a big hotel, Mr. Wallops. Sometimes we have unanticipated needs.

SERGIO

I'll do that.

(Exits.)

LOOGEY
(To TENANT)

Find out who that nincompoop is.

TENANT

No need, boss. That's Sergio Pack, son of the botanical Packs. Calls himself an actor, but he's never performed before, not even in a high school skit. Good chance we've just witnessed his debut.

LOOGEY

The kid thinks he's Batman, so far as I know. I don't want him snooping the roost. Anyone else, I'd say harvest him to be safe, but I don't wanna cross swords without cause against the Department.

TENANT

How about we make him an accessory? Pair him up with a black ring, an intimidation job. Make it so he touches nothing but gets an eyeful, enough to know what happens to those who make trouble. Messy so he gets queasy for the work, but standing far enough away that he doesn't dirty his fingers in the soup.

LOOGEY

You got someone who can handle a job like that?

TENANT

Philip Humphrey, boss. When you talk to him, he's a regular guy. But when he's working, I don't think he's quite human. Professional, though. Does what you ask of him, dirty as you ask, and not a mote more.

LOOGEY

See that it's done.

(LOOGEY and TENANT exit.)

(BLACKOUT)

SCENE two

(SETTING: A squalid studio apartment.)

(AT RISE: HUMPHREY and SERGIO gearing up for an intimidation job.)

HUMPHREY
Did you bring a weapon?
          (SERGIO produces a Napoleonic era Nock pistol)
That relic?

SERGIO
Pardon me, it's an *antique*. My parents keep the relics in a whole other room.

HUMPHREY
      (Inspecting)
You may not fire this around me. The recoil alone might shatter someone's face. Here, take mine.
      (Hands over a gun)

SERGIO

But I don't know how to use this.

HUMPHREY
(Demonstrating)

Chamber. Fire. I need you armed. There probably won't be any violence, but sometimes people don't get the message. If that happens—chances slim but distinctly non-zero—I will give you this signal.

(Gestures)

Following so far?

SERGIO

Yes.

HUMPHREY

In which case, you unholster the gun and fire one—can you count to one?—exactly one warning shot. Don't worry, the walls in the room will be cinder blocks, they'll absorb the round.

SERGIO

Hmm? Oh right, people on the other side.

HUMPHREY

The key is you do not strike the target. More importantly, you do not strike me. Capitskay?

SERGIO

Capito.

HUMPHREY

What's the matter? Comments, complaints?

SERGIO

No. I was just hoping I wouldn't have to do anything I could go to jail for. Not on the first gig.

HUMPHREY

Listen, Sergio, in Dodoville, we are a civilized people. Mob intimidation is ritualized and polite. I merely inform the target I am the individual who fills newly-emptied eye sockets with sawdust. That's it. I don't say *your* eye sockets. Usually I don't even show them the spoon.

SERGIO

The?

HUMPHREY

I use a spoon; the surface area leverages better and it's rusty. Point is, we conduct the business like gentlemen. Mere formalities.

SERGIO

So why the gun?

HUMPHREY

For those who don't comply with company protocol, we fire a shot across the bow. But don't worry: police consider it parcel to ordinary business transactions.

SERGIO

What, death threats?

HUMPHREY

(Dismissively)

Words, words.

SERGIO

Except a gunshot.

    (A knock at the door)

Company!

HUMPHREY

Sergio, this is a two-man job, and you're less than one yet.

    (Enter NOODLE, large and muscular, with a two-liter soda bottle and a tub of ice cream.)

NOODLE

    (His voice sing-song)

Who wants root beer floats?

    (Bear hugs HUMPHREY, holding the ice cream against the back of his neck.)

HUMPHREY

    (Struggling free)

Jesus, that's cold.

NOODLE

Cold as your heart, you murderous bastard!

HUMPHREY

    (Humorless)

Excuse me. Dispenser of justified force during high level security operations.

NOODLE

Too bad. I only trust murderous men. Do you have any spoons?

    (HUMPHREY shows him his spoon)

Sick fuck.

rhadamanthus

    (Points at SERGIO)
Who's the sandbag?

      HUMPHREY
Forrest Wallops.
    (To SERGIO)
And this one, not even he remembers his real name. Call him Noodle.

      NOODLE
Because I used to farm catfish barehanded.

      HUMPHREY
He means he once put his fist down a man's throat for no more than his dinner.

      NOODLE
Those were lean years, don't judge a man. My thumb-finger ain't as black as some's.

      HUMPHREY
Still a shade too much darker than the rest of you. Me, I'd have you put out to pasture.

      NOODLE
    (Giggling)
Good you ain't ganglord yet! I'm too poor to retire.

      HUMPHREY
Not to graze, but to be grazed upon.

      NOODLE
    (Making a sad face)
Aw. Too poor even to die.

HUMPHREY
The fee you're taking tonight, you could buy a kingdom and settle down.

NOODLE
I wish.

HUMPHREY
Like Spain.

NOODLE
Too small for a man like me. See, I've got these habits.

HUMPHREY
That so? Maybe Mr. Wallops here can help you out. He's into botany.

NOODLE
Botany! Oh my.
    (To SERGIO)
Your next pushjob, you'll be showing spoons to me!

SERGIO
My parents are scientists.

NOODLE
    (Surprised)
If your family has science money, what are you doing getting your thumb blackened?

SERGIO
Some things money can't buy.

NOODLE
Like what?

rhadamanthus

SERGIO

A career in the arts.

NOODLE

(Laughing)

Humphrey, wherever you dug up this smartass, I like him.

HUMPHREY

Enough chitchat. Noodle, you're the muscle tonight.

NOODLE

That must make you the charm! Life's a comedy.
    (Pointing at SERGIO, who's still holding the weapon)
What's his pose then? Arsenal?

HUMPHREY

(to NOODLE, flexing)

Take your coat off, show us those guns. Then give it to Mr. Wallops, so he can hide his.

NOODLE

Listen, we're all friends here, but if the new guy's toting, so am I.
    (Takes his coat off and lays it on SERGIO's shoulders)
You're making a horrible mistake, kid. That's all the talking you out of it I'm gonna to do.

SERGIO

Is the life really that bad?

NOODLE

(Starts to say something but thinks better of it)

Roll up the sleeves. Make 'em afraid you'll cut 'em with those elbows.

HUMPHREY
(To NOODLE)
You look slippery as a duck now. Try on my hat, for gravity.
(Places a fedora with a large silver medallion on NOODLE's head)

NOODLE
These fists have gravity enough.

HUMPHREY
Keep 'em in your pockets. A stage show, this. Just look the part.

NOODLE
(Studying the mirror)
The ass I look, I wouldn't get caught dead in this. Who's the holy spook on the medal?

HUMPHREY
St Jude, patron of lost causes.

NOODLE
Jude my ass. Fucker weighs a ton.
(Turns a fearsome face to the others)
Nobody who doesn't eat a root beer float with me gets out this room alive.

HUMPHREY
S'why you weigh a fucking ton.

NOODLE
Muscle. You said so yourself.

HUMPHREY
Let's head out.

rhadamanthus

(to SERGIO)

Mr. Wallops, if you plan on looking intimidating tonight, you better start now.

(BLACKOUT)

SCENE three

(SETTING: Office of Labor Union President, BILLIE PARLIAMENT. Prominent wall photo of stevedores awaiting a shipment.)

(AT RISE: PARLIAMENT at her desk, whistling merrily as she counts cash.)

(Knock at the door. HUMPHREY enters with NOODLE and SERGIO, as Forrest Wallops.)

HUMPHREY
Billie Parliament. I'm Philip Humphrey, I represent Samson Loogey. May my associates and I step inside?

PARLIAMENT
(Eying HUMPHREY, confused)
Philip?

rhadamanthus

HUMPHREY
(Irritably)
Humphrey. Yes, Ms. Parliament.

PARLIAMENT
To what do I owe the pleasure?

HUMPHREY
Social call. Now that Loogey Sr. has passed, his heir wants to press palms with his father's old contacts, to prevent close friendships from becoming passing strangerships.

PARLIAMENT
Tell the young Mr. Loogey I'll miss his father deeply. Although we often disagreed, he understood the need for concord between the aluminum workers' union and himself. For that, I respected him, and I'm proud if he considered me a friend as well as a rival, as I certainly regarded him. I look forward to making closer acquaintance with the son of such a man.

HUMPHREY
My employer has asked me to extend similar sentiments. As a gesture of goodwill, he wants to inform you he's lifted the unfortunate hiring freeze which the recent economic downturn had made unavoidable.

PARLIAMENT
(Surprised)
Indeed! I hadn't expected to hear that for a few months. This is good news.

HUMPHREY
In exchange, I need something from you.

PARLIAMENT
In exchange? For returning the factories to full output?

HUMPHREY

Unfortunately, as the union's advocate, you've done your job too well. The senior loomies have become too expensive to compensate for their labor. These days the entire industry is in jeopardy. To preserve it, we need to arrange for the immediate layoff of all machine laborers scheduled to retire in the next five years.

PARLIAMENT

(Startled)

I don't have to tell you the union council will never agree to that. They'd sooner extend the hiring freeze.

HUMPHREY

Mr. Loogey understands this policy will be disagreeable, yet it is necessary. Here is in fact where he requires your assistance.

PARLIAMENT

What are you getting at?

HUMPHREY

You must convince the layoffs not to file claims against their pensions. As a form of protest and a leveraging tactic.

PARLIAMENT

(Outraged)

On pretext of accomplishing what?

HUMPHREY

Generating public sympathy. The city is fiercely loyal to its loomy heritage. After a public showdown, Mr. Loogey will grant an expansion of their benefits, in exchange for their early retirement. A victory for the union, a gesture of generosity for Mr. Loogey, and the solvency of the factories ensured.

rhadamanthus

PARLIAMENT

And how long will this carry on? What incentive can I offer the workers you want to force into retirement not to draw on their pensions either? They have families to think of.

HUMPHREY

(A note of malice in his voice)

It's concern for their families which drives this request. The pension fund has been adversely affected by the recent downturn, and now there is an additional complication.

PARLIAMENT

(Suspicious)

What complication?

(A pause)

HUMPHREY

Economic constraints are forcing us to consolidate the extended Loogey organization into the aluminum family.

PARLIAMENT

You don't mean your thugs!

HUMPHREY

I mean the employees of Black Ring Security Services.

PARLIAMENT

They work for the factory now? You're calling them security!

HUMPHREY

That has always been their function. They protect Mr. Loogey's interests in Dodoville, first and foremost the aluminum plant.

PARLIAMENT

Mr. Loogey Sr. and I had an ironclad agreement about this: the aluminum output could only be guaranteed so long as he kept his extracurriculars off the factory floor. Legitimate loomy labor is certainly not going to share workspace with—

HUMPHREY

Not just workspace. The black rings will now draw salary from the same fund as the loomy pensions.

PARLIAMENT

What?! That money can't be commingled.

HUMPHREY

Yes, it can, legally. All it takes is the signature of the Aluminum Labor Union President.

PARLIAMENT

Forget it.

HUMPHREY

(Casually)

This is a dangerous city. Black Ring Security Services are here for your protection. Other industrialists in Dodoville are not as charitable or even-tempered as Mr. Loogey. Among them are saboteurs, makers of unfortunate accidents. Without their protection—

PARLIAMENT

What the workers need is protection from the black rings!

HUMPHREY

(Smug)

rhadamanthus

Honestly? I couldn't agree more. Because think what would happen if these hardworking security personnel tried to draw pay for services so diligently performed, only to find their checks bounced because a certain union felt too fancy to drink from the same bowl. Men who risk personal welfare during these dangerous times for the safety of those very same workers.

PARLIAMENT
(Bitterly)
I don't recall anyone asking for their assistance.

HUMPHREY
If Black Ring employees should go unpaid, Mr. Loogey cannot guarantee the safety of the loomy pension holders—

PARLIAMENT
If you came in here claiming to be the late Mr. Loogey's representative, I would have assumed you were a fraud.

HUMPHREY
(Leaning forward and speaking more softly)
—or the safety of the pension holders' beneficiaries.

PARLIAMENT
Out. I refuse to discuss this under these conditions. Tell Samson Loogey to take this insanity before the union council if he dares! He is not going to manage it quietly with any backroom deal.

HUMPHREY
Noodle. Hold her down.

NOODLE
(Rubbing his hands)
Honest work for an honest wage. A man can take pleasure in it.
(Pins PARLIAMENT.)

PARLIAMENT

(Frightened)

What are you doing? Hurting me won't get me what you want.

HUMPHREY

I don't see why not.

PARLIAMENT

Help! Murder, murder!

HUMPHREY

(Produces papers)

No, not yet. Only if we can't persuade you to sign this document.

PARLIAMENT

(With fear in her voice)

You're deluded if you imagine the people I represent are not more dangerous than you. I shudder to think what blood would be spilled if I signed that.

HUMPHREY

It's true. We're not more dangerous, Ms. Parliament. But I'm afraid we are much more immediate. Your signature, please.

PARLIAMENT

(Spitting)

Go to hell. I'd rather die upholding the oaths I've sworn.

HUMPHREY

Mr. Wallops. Place your weapon against this woman's forehead.

SERGIO

W-w-

rhadamanthus

HUMPHREY

Did I say stutter? Unholster your firearm and put it between her eyes.
    (SERGIO complies, shaking)
Do you wish to reconsider, Ms. Parliament?

SERGIO

This is not what—

PARLIAMENT

This changes nothing. You have nothing to threaten me with. Kill me if you must. See where it gets you.

HUMPHREY

Very well. Fire, Mr. Wallops.
    (SERGIO hesitates, then pulls the gun away.)
Did you not hear me? Mr. Wallops! Address your weapon to this woman's forehead and squeeze the trigger.
    (Gives the agreed-upon signal)

NOODLE

    (As he adjusts his hat, the medal on the band gleams.
    His voice is sorrowful.)
Make the right career move, kid.

PARLIAMENT

Sergio. Does your mother—

    (SERGIO steps back and covers his eyes. Raising the gun, he fires once. NOODLE's head explodes, splattering gore across the faces of the other three. SERGIO screams and drops the weapon. Released, PARLIAMENT regains her feet and retrieves a machete from the wall.)

HUMPHREY

(To SERGIO)

Imbecile! What have you done? Son of a bitch, what have you done!

SERGIO

I didn't. I don't. I have no idea wh—

HUMPHREY

(To SERGIO)

Out of here. Now.

(To PARLIAMENT)

This is not the end of this.

PARLIAMENT

You are damn right!

HUMPHREY

(To SERGIO)

Move it.

(HUMPHREY and SERGIO exit, leaving NOODLE to bleed out on the floor.)

(BLACKOUT)

SCENE four

(SETTING: An alleyway outside loomy union headquarters.)

(AT RISE: SERGIO enters running, covered in brains. HUMPHREY walks behind him, casually cleaning himself off.)

SERGIO

I shot him. Oh God, Humphrey, I shot that man's face off.

HUMPHREY
(Calmly)
The side of his head, actually. The face only looks missing on account of the gore.

SERGIO

You said nobody would get hurt! This was only supposed to be intimidation. Nobody was gonna get hurt!

HUMPHREY
You fired a gun with your eyes closed in a room full of people. It could've been worse.

SERGIO
W-w-

HUMPHREY
Catching him in the head was lucky. If you'd just winged him, there's no telling what he would have done. He's called Noodle for a reason.

SERGIO
Is it . . . Are we sure he's dead?

HUMPHREY
(Snorting)
I told you not to get involved, Mr. Wallops.

SERGIO
Loogey is going to be furious when he finds out.

HUMPHREY
Loogey will have you killed. He has no choice. But it may be even worse than that.

SERGIO
W-w-

HUMPHREY
Worse. Billie Parliament recognized you, didn't she?

SERGIO
Not that I . . .

rhadamanthus

HUMPHREY

She called you Sergio, Mr. Wallops. She asked about your mother.

SERGIO

I—So? Everyone has a—

HUMPHREY

Which means Samson Loogey is about to find out you're a blood relation of his gangland rival. So when Loogey hears what you did to Noodle, he'll assume you are a mole in his organization, and that you've begun murdering his men on behalf of the University of Dodoville's botany department.

SERGIO

It was an accident!

HUMPHREY

Who cares? Once word gets out, Samson will need to make an example of you to save face. By the way: here, "example" means gruesome.

SERGIO

I'm going to get the spoon!

HUMPHREY

You should be so fortunate. If Loogey doesn't bloody his pliers on you, gangland will believe he can't protect his own people. That he lacks leadership.

SERGIO

(Slumps to the ground)

I'm going to die. They are going to torture me to death. In hideous, freakish, agonizing ways. I just wanted to be in a play.

HUMPHREY
(Sits beside SERGIO, his voice softening)

Listen. First and foremost, Loogey will have to retaliate against the Department or risk looking weak. They are no trifling adversary—listen!—and in the ruckus that follows there's a chance he may overlook coming after you personally. If, that is, someone powerful makes a show of protecting you.

SERGIO

I can't go to my parents.

HUMPHREY
(Instantly)

No. Because the Department Chair will surrender you as a peace offering—

SERGIO

Mom?

HUMPHREY

Yes, Mr. Wallops. Your mother knows even if her botanists can win this fight, a battle against the black rings now will weaken the Department in the long term. And she won't let anything get in the way of her plans for this city, not even her only son!

SERGIO
(Sobbing)

I'm even more worthless than science!

HUMPHREY

You can, however, seek asylum from Rhadamanthus Flynn.

SERGIO

W-w-

rhadamanthus

HUMPHREY

Who.
    (Whispering)
He's a man who really does have moles in the Loogey organization. And he plans to take it over. Your only chance might be to wager that Flynn's coup of Loogey aluminum will be successful.

SERGIO

Will it?

HUMPHREY

    (Shrugging)
If I were you, I'd seek him out. Say you've murdered a black ring and you want protection. If he decides to trust you, he'll make you an operative. It's dangerous work, but at least you'll have a chance to fight for your life.

SERGIO

I just wanted to be in a play!

HUMPHREY

We all just wanted things.
    (Stands and helps SERGIO to his feet)
Now run. The police will be here in a minute, and you look a man who's just blown somebody's brains out.

    (SERGIO exits.)

    (Enter FLYNN in lavish evening dress.)

HUMPHREY

It's done, Flynn. Noodle is dead.
    (Hands FLYNN a device)

will madden

This remote detonated an explosive on his hat, concealed as a miraculous medal. Sergio Pack believes he shot him. And once Billie Parliament talks, Loogey and his organization will believe it too. Aluminum will be forced to declare war on the Department.

FLYNN
(Studying the remote)
A risky plan. I wasn't sure you could pull it off.

HUMPHREY
You didn't have to worry.

FLYNN
The Department is stronger than Loogey realizes. It's going to be a massacre.

HUMPHREY
After the botanists finish seizing territory, there won't be much left for us.

FLYNN
While the war rages, we'll move in and lay claim to the aluminum plant itself. It's been the seat of power in this city for a long time, and that's not about to change.

HUMPHREY
But what if the botanists prefer to see it turned into a riverside park?

FLYNN
Professor Pack has ceded me the plant in exchange for my signature on a new contract. To purchase the Department's new commercial product in bulk.

HUMPHREY
(Whispers)
Poisons!

rhadamanthus

FLYNN

Think of them as vials of persuasion.

HUMPHREY

How do you know the Department Chair won't try to persuade you too?

FLYNN

(Defiant)

Because I now own her son. She may be a ruthless power player, but when it comes to the men in her life, she's as sentimental as river moonlight.

HUMPHREY

Aluminum has been the heart of this city for generations. Aren't you worried about the chaos if the industry is dismantled too quickly?

FLYNN

The collapse is already inevitable, the jengaists have seen to that. But now, Samson Loogey will go down knowing the reason he's being punished.

(A moment.)

HUMPHREY

Which is what, if I may ask?

FLYNN

(Darkly)

You have your business, I have mine.

HUMPHREY

Some black rings are saying you hate Samson because you're Chancel's bastard, and you begrudge this other son his inheritance.

FLYNN

    (Unreadable)

Do you believe that?

HUMPHREY

    (Resolutely)

I believe that you and I have an agreement, and I've just carried out my end.

FLYNN

And I'm satisfied with the result. Don't worry, you'll have your chance to obtain the justice you seek.

HUMPHREY

I better. My twin sister's fury cries out for vengeance.

    (Quietly)

Mara Carpenter's death must be repaid in blood.

FLYNN

Then rest assured! Even now, my agents snap at Rico Daggett's fleeing heels. Your soul's disquiet won't plague you much longer.

HUMPHREY

For the record, Flynn: Noodle was a friend of mine.

FLYNN

    (Surprised, searching)

I'll be happy to list his crimes if it'll make you feel better. But if you wanted to plead for his life, the time was *before* you blew his head off.

HUMPHREY

Just speaking for the record.

rhadamanthus

FLYNN

Noted.

(FLYNN and HUMPHREY regard each other in silence.)

(HUMPHREY exits.)

(FLYNN takes a deep breath and flips a coin. He sighs in relief at the result. A nervous smile as he exits.)

(CURTAIN)

ACT four
SCENE one

(SETTING: The present, 1987. The stage of the Mountebank Theater done up as the lobby of the Denmark Hotel. Mirrored walls, a grand stairway, a large fountain in which eels can be seen to swim. By whatever logic, the volcanic dome of Mount Myrtle looms in the background.)

(AT RISE: CLAUDIUS the king, GERTRUDE the queen, LAERTES, and SERGIO as Hamlet lie slain aside the fountain. CLAUDIUS, no longer dead, struggles out from under Polonius' cloak and calls for help as the lights slowly dim.)

CLAUDIUS

Help! Help! Help!

rhadamanthus

(The Danish court disappears into darkness)

SERGIO
(As Hamlet)
And the rest is silence.

(No applause. After a moment, lights come on. The cast begins to stir as the STAGE CREW rushes to prepare for DAGGETT's farewell performance in two hours. As the STAGE MANAGER shouts directions, equipment begins to move. CLAUDIUS and GERTRUDE are carried off as if props.)

GERTRUDE
(In character)
Hands off, man. We are not a stool!

(SERGIO rises amid the ruckus. Stage blood remains on his hands and sleeves. He dodges SHOWGIRLS as they rehearse last-minute changes to choreography.)

(Enter DAGGETT, attended by HUMPHREY in glasses. DAGGETT converses with PLINKO the director; he touches fellow PERFORMERS warmly on the shoulder as they pass.)

(Enter GOONS 1 & 2, dressed as stage crew, carrying clay pots. As they and HUMPHREY bump into each other, a pot falls. HUMPHREY removes his glasses to speak as GOONS sweep up the mess.)

HUMPHREY
I trust your men are assembled?

GOON 1

And eager! Awaiting word to lay siege to this theater.

GOON 2

And strangle it with tendrils of their rage.

HUMPHREY

Excellent! Tonight in Dodoville, Botany enters full bloom.

GOON 2

Humphrey, your years of service to the Department have been unshakable alike onto an oak. But what of Daggett?

HUMPHREY

I've spread rumor about town that Flynn will have him slain upon stage tonight. You can't score a ticket in Dodoville anywhere!

GOON 1

People say to the scalpers, "Take as much off the top as you wish, just leave me the eyes to see it!"

HUMPHREY

When the curtain rises on Daggett already dead, they'll want revenge for the stolen spectacle.

GOON 2

Undoubtedly! For three years, Flynn has whet their appetite for Daggett's mournful end.

GOON 1

Most like they'll slake their sanguine thirst on Flynn himself when his finale leaves them dry!

rhadamanthus

HUMPHREY

At worst, he'll lose public support. And without it, the Department's war against him is all but won.

GOON 1

But the assassin? Can we trust he'll strike home on cue?

(HUMPHREY and GOONS glance at SERGIO, who bumbles around, lost.)

HUMPHREY

(Drawing a dagger)

I swear by this hand, you'll see murder done. Await my signal, then come forth leafy!

GOON 2

When?

HUMPHREY

(Sheathing the knife)

An hour. Before the orchestra's tuned.

GOON 1

By then he'll have sung his final note.

GOON 2

Sour as death!

HUMPHREY

But sweet to our ears. Go now.

(GOONS exit. HUMPHREY catches SERGIO's eye and waves him over. On the way, SERGIO is jostled by STAGE CREW.)

SERGIO
(Too loudly, eying DAGGETT)

Hey, Humphrey! About setting that fire to a certain someone's hotel room. I'm going to need your help.

HUMPHREY

Shh!
(Muffling SERGIO)

Here's your first lesson: Rico Daggett does not intend to perform tonight. He senses something amiss and plans to flee before the curtain goes up.

SERGIO
(Alarmed)

We have to tell Flynn.

HUMPHREY

Unwise. Fulfilling this contract is your only means of repaying your debt to him. If he bails you out now, you'll remain indentured to him forever.

SERGIO

So, what do I do?

HUMPHREY

You'll have to improvise.
(Shows SERGIO the dagger)

SERGIO
(Confused)

Improvise how? Stab Daggett in the leg so he can't run?

HUMPHREY

With your luck, you'll snag an artery. Amazing how fast a man can bleed out.

rhadamanthus

SERGIO

(Rueful)

Flynn wants the show to go off tonight. I can't afford to kill anyone else by mistake.

HUMPHREY

(Chuckling)

The newspapers would love it. "Mad Hamlet's Backstage Murder." You could claim artist's insanity as a legal defense.

SERGIO

(Panicked)

I should flee too, if Daggett does.

HUMPHREY

Flynn will find you, like he found Daggett. Your only hope is to keep him here till after the show, so you can fulfill your contract.

(PHOTOGRAPHERS gather as DAGGETT kneels before a framed photo of Mara and makes the sign of the cross. One REPORTER narrates into a video camera.)

SERGIO

(Pointing toward DAGGETT)

That's been his pre-show schtick since his return from exile. I wonder if he actually prays.

HUMPHREY

He might. He's performed this show over four hundred times—reliving his wife's death, over and over and over. Tonight it ends, all the To Mara and To Mara. Tonight it sinks in that Mara will never come.

SERGIO

But is he praying?

HUMPHREY

(Delighted, rubbing his hands)

To be spared from the eels, I promise you! Ooh, they scare him so much!

SERGIO

For forgiveness, I mean. Did he really kill his wife? If so, is he sorry? You must know something by now, you've been with him so long.

HUMPHREY

(Nodding)

Every night for the last three years. I put him to bed and wake him in the morning. I usher mistresses in and out of his rooms; endure his coke-fueled bragging and drunken sobbing; answer his phone, do his laundry, drive his cars; barber and shave him, massaged his body; administer injections, pluck hairs, pop zits. I'm more his wife than Mara Carpenter ever was! I know everything one human being can know about another.

SERGIO

And?

(For a moment, it seems there will be no answer.)

HUMPHREY

You can barely get him in the bath, he's so terrified of water. But you might say that's as easily the result of losing Mara at sea as the cause of it.
  (A SHOWGIRL helps DAGGETT to his feet. He
  kisses her on the cheek. The kiss seems formal but
  familiar. Together they pose for a photograph.)
He watches your play, you know, from the balcony.
  (SERGIO perks up.)

Not to see you. The cave diver they got to play Ophelia. The scene where they find her body in the fountain. Floating face down in the water.

SERGIO

Every night the audience holds its breath with her. You hear gasps of air around the theater as their lungs give out.

HUMPHREY

Daggett started that. It's a kind of ritual for him.

SERGIO

When they finally pull her out, her chest still doesn't rise. She's got lungs the size of bed pillows.

HUMPHREY

He likes to chat up the actress after the show. It makes him feel better to see she's still alive.

SERGIO

They say Anna can't stand him. But also . . .

HUMPHREY

(Angry, almost defensive)
She only slept with him 'cause she thought he'd leave her alone afterward.

SERGIO

The eels make me anxious. Being in the tank with her body. They're supposed to be poisonous.

HUMPHREY

(Uncharacteristically fidgety)
You're too young to remember, but Flynn has Ophelia dress like Mara. The outfit she wore in her most famous Hollywood role.

(ANNA sits beside the fountain and feeds the eels by hand. The AQUARIUM KEEPER demands that she stop. She pleads, but the KEEPER remains adamant.)

SERGIO

"Yes, my good lord." "No, my good lord." Even with lines like that, Anna has them written inside her sleeve, just in case.

HUMPHREY

The Jaunting Carriage. That's the name of the film. Mara played Sophia Lauren's best friend. I bet nobody could even tell you the character's name. But that dress is how everyone remembers her. How beautiful she was in it.

SERGIO

Anna says she misses the cave monsters. From the pools where she used to dive in Mexico. I wonder if there really are monsters down there. And if they're friendly.

HUMPHREY

Mara only appeared in four Hollywood films, but she left Dodoville's most inedible mark on cinema. When they think of our city around the world, they think of Mara Carpenter.

SERGIO

The earth's full of wonders nobody knows about! So why not the sea creature Daggett says he saw the day Mara died? That notorious jellyfish? Once science classifies it, it's just an animal. Monsters stop existing the moment you prove they're real.

(DAGGETT walks over to the fountain and sits. Without looking at him, ANNA gets up and leaves.

rhadamanthus

DAGGETT studies the eels, keeping a distance from the glass.)

HUMPHREY
Your job right now is to convince him to perform tonight. Prevent his escape so you can murder him after the show.

(Moments pass.)

SERGIO
How?

HUMPHREY
Get him to feel himself in fully in the moment. Remember, his greatest fear is he'll never stand upon a stage again. Remind him how he can't survive without the adoration of a crowd.

SERGIO
I guess. I just wish he and I had more in common.

(DAGGETT takes out a book and reads.)

(Enter FLYNN. He glowers at HUMPHREY, who nods in acknowledgment.)

HUMPHREY
I've no time to walk you through this. Trust your instincts. Don't forget: the expression on your face is warm, the steel in your hand stays cold.
(Turns to leave)

SERGIO
(Calling)
What if I can't do it?

HUMPHREY
(Calling back)
Then you'll never act again!
(Stands beside FLYNN. They whisper to each other.)

SERGIO
How wicked to approach him in friendship while harboring a dagger in my heart! Well, whatever: I will close the book of my thoughts so he cannot read intent in the lines of my brow. But will he suspect me? I doubt he even knows my name.
(HUMPHREY nods to FLYNN and exits.)
Hey, wait up! One quick question!

(SERGIO exits, following.)

SCENE two

(SETTING: Unbroken from before.)

(AT RISE: FLYNN and DAGGETT are alone on stage. DAGGETT reads his book. He has not looked at FLYNN, who stands behind him.)

DAGGETT
Hey Flynn. I was just thumbing through *The Absolute Imbecile's Guide to Sitting Through the Mountebank's Insufferable Hamlet*. Have you seen this?

FLYNN
(Peering at the cover)
Looks likes the instruction manual to a household appliance.

DAGGETT

Yeah, a coffee pot. Since we lost the war, these are the only things the Americans allow us to print. So Dodoville's writers smuggle their screeds in them.

FLYNN

It's not the Americans. If I didn't suppress subversive literature in this town, this occupation would be much worse. It's for everyone's own good.

DAGGETT

(Skeptical)

Speaking of tyrants. The uh . . .

(Glances at the cover)

The "Herr Kaffeetrinken XE" wants to know why your play tries to make us feel so bad for the king when he cries "Help help" at the end. Since it's his crimes that are responsible for the whole rotten state to begin with. A sensible person might think it's a happy ending.

FLYNN

(Softly)

I think the play is misread. I think the true subject is the tragedy of King Claudius.

DAGGETT

Oh, you would!

FLYNN

(With dignity)

And of Denmark. Too-soon deprived of a wise ruler.

DAGGETT

A pretty free interpretation, don't you think?

rhadamanthus

FLYNN

Not at all. The kingdom enjoys a brokered peace, a court full of entertainments—

DAGGETT

That's one way to polish a turd.

FLYNN

Art and prosperity. What more can you ask for?

DAGGETT

Well—and this is me spitballing here—maybe fewer murder plots? Because, myself, I feel less safe around them.

(The two meet eyes in a meaningful exchange.)

FLYNN

Establishing and maintaining order is sometimes unpleasant. But Claudius performs it clinically, like an act of political hygiene.

DAGGETT

Hygiene!

FLYNN

As dirty hands must be scrubbed for the health of the organism, so must the body politic. To do less is slovenly and unwholesome. So yes, Mr. Daggett, hygiene.

DAGGETT

Scrubbing the skin is fine, but what about bleaching your own blood?

FLYNN

What do you mean?

DAGGETT

Nothing. Only some say in Denmark, just like Dodoville, the bossman came to power by playing his predecessor most foully.
    (In a whisper)
A man believed to be his own brother.

FLYNN
    (Surprised by the comment)
Whatever you are implying, Samson Loogey is still alive.

DAGGETT

Technically. But Loogey's been on hard times since he fell from his aluminum pedestal. Death might have been better.

FLYNN

That is not my business.

DAGGETT

No? Seems like all his business is yours now!

FLYNN

Claudius was more fit to rule, but his brother was the legal heir. Should the state be held hostage to accidents of birth?

DAGGETT

I don't know who's better fit, but I can say who was better suited.
    (Points at FLYNN's pants)
Just look at those slacks! Power could afford a tailor, I thought.

FLYNN

To argue the superiority of the late king over Claudius, Hamlet appeals to their portraits. This one so handsome, that one so oafish. Because he believes, as fools do, that quality of character is in the face, not the fortitude.

rhadamanthus

DAGGETT

(Glancing at FLYNN's messy hair)

What about the follicles? Haven't you ever heard of a comb?

FLYNN

What Samson merely inherited, I fought for. Against this city's most brutal ganglords, armed with only a bell.

DAGGETT

Well, you showed everybody! Now you are another ganglord, no different than them. Another criminal.

FLYNN

The custodian of the state.

DAGGETT

Well. Careful you don't end with a belly full of poison and steel.

FLYNN

Excuse me?

DAGGETT

Like Claudius.

FLYNN

What are his final words? This is key. "Yet defend me friends, I am but hurt." An attempt to make the next viable move, even as the blade pierces him. To respond with the same composure, the same drive toward success, that characterized the rest of his life.

DAGGETT

Not me. Once I feel death's edge, I'm taking the rest of the night off.

FLYNN

Because you have no character.

DAGGETT

Why have one? I am one.

FLYNN

(Smiling faintly)

In the real world, the play would end differently. For one, a man like Claudius would never have met his end through Hamlet, not even by accident.

(Placing a hand tiredly to his forehead)

More likely it results from fatigue, a fatal accumulation of tiny errors over time. Until one day . . .

DAGGETT

I'd be interested in seeing that play!

FLYNN

Stick around.

DAGGETT

No, I wouldn't. Sounds too long.

(A hard smile)

Only if I could skip right to the end.

FLYNN

(A touch of whimsy)

For some, the end comes almost as a relief, doesn't it?

DAGGETT

(Closing his eyes, a wave of pain shuddering through him)

To Mara and to Mara.

rhadamanthus

(FLYNN and DAGGETT exchange an almost sympathetic look.)

Samson Loogey never tortured me on stage for three years, that's all I'm saying.

FLYNN
(His mood turning)

Was it torture for you? Good heavens, I didn't suspect!

DAGGETT

The man who knows everything.

FLYNN

Well, you earn your freedom tonight.

DAGGETT

Oh, do I? What a relief!

FLYNN

I honor my bargains.

DAGGETT

So does the devil! The letter of it, at least.

(FLYNN turns away.)

Listen, whatever I've done to offend you—which is nothing, by the way, except call you an unkempt vulture to your face—why don't we skip all this tonight?

FLYNN

Skip the show? Impossible.

DAGGETT

Don't be coy. I mean how 'bout we give a pass to my whole execution thing?

(Finding the nerve not to look away)
In light of all the money I've made you. Why shouldn't I enjoy a sprinkle of retirement to flavor my hard-earned freedom?

FLYNN
(Not without compassion.)
Where would you go, Rico? What's even the point of you without a stage? Remember when I found you at the end of the world? You said you'd let Dodoville roast you like a pig if only you could sing for them while they turned the spit.

DAGGETT
It was freezing in that little shack. The fantasy was more about the heat than the applause.

FLYNN
I know what's in your heart.

DAGGETT
Me too. A knife, in about an hour.

FLYNN
You don't know how to feel loved without being in pain. You never could. I only gave you want you really wanted.

DAGGETT
So listen, Mr. Claudius the King, then give me this. Hamlet gets a chance to cross swords for his life. Shouldn't I? One last show. Private, for your eyes only. Him and me. My executioner. To the death.

FLYNN
(Snorts)
Is that all you want? There.

(Points toward where SERGIO enters with HUMPHREY)
That is the man with the poison on his blade. Aren't I a benevolent king?

DAGGETT

(Almost insulted)

Him? I thought you'd show me my better. That overgrown child I can best with my eyes closed.

FLYNN

Any way you like! Send Humphrey with a message when it's finished.
(Turns to leave)

DAGGETT

(Anxious)

Don't you wanna see how it turns out?

FLYNN

(Shrugging)

I've spent months orchestrating tonight. With my whole career on the line, I've been assigning roles to everyone, making sure they act their part. You're the only one I know will perform his perfectly.

DAGGETT

Humphrey said the same thing this morning. Why does everyone think I'm so predictable?

FLYNN

(Scoffing)

Sheer stupidity, must be.

DAGGETT

You look worried.

FLYNN

(Rubbing his hands anxiously)

Excited! Tonight my erstwhile allies come to betray me. But the trap is set. When it springs . . . A spectacle to live in this city's memory forever! No one will ever forget the name Rhadamanthus!

DAGGETT

If they can pronounce it! But listen, I do in fact have a trick or two left up my sleeve.

FLYNN

(A wry smile)

Show me! I enjoy a surprise. Look, here comes your murderer. Slay him first if it suits you!

(SERGIO approaches with HUMPHREY)

SERGIO

(Noticing DAGGETT's book)

What are we reading?

DAGGETT

Notes on a coffee pot.

FLYNN

May I?

(Takes the booklet)

Oh, Humphrey, you'll enjoy this part.

(Reads)

"Laertes returns to Denmark, vowing to avenge his slaughtered father *and drowned sister.*

(Feigning surprise at the coincidence, he glances mockingly at HUMPHREY, who looks away.)

rhadamanthus

But what of his resolve? He grovels to ask the king's permission to perform the deed which is his blood's duty. From there, only disaster ensues. He ends up crushed in the gears of that sovereign's nefarious machinations."

(HUMPHREY removes his glasses as if to argue, glances at DAGGETT, then restores them.)

HUMPHREY

Forgive me, sir. I don't remember the play. Is the villain not slain? Does that sister's sibling not avenge her by his own hand?

FLYNN

Only barely. He nearly misses his chance. Then dies begging for forgiveness like a coward.

HUMPHREY

Then that's how you know it's Shakespeare, sir. In Dodoville it would different.

FLYNN

That remains to be seen.

SERGIO

(Totally confused)

Seen by who? What are we talking about?

DAGGETT

(Also perplexed)

Who knows? I just learned there's some betrayal at the theater tonight. Maybe it's something to do with that?

(HUMPHREY flashes a look at DAGGETT)

                    FLYNN
         (Grabbing HUMPHREY roughly by the elbow)
Mr. Daggett, I need to borrow Humphrey for a moment. Perhaps my two brightest stars care to know each other a little better before one's light fades from the stage?

              (HUMPHREY nods to SERGIO)

                    SERGIO
         (Anxious)
I'd appreciate the opportunity.

                    HUMPHREY
         (To DAGGETT)
Sir, I'll return to attend to you shortly.
              (To SERGIO, he mimes the thrust of a dagger)

              (Exits, removing glasses.)

                    FLYNN
Remember, Pack: heaven can wait, but hell is in a hurry.

              (Winks at DAGGETT. Exits.)

SCENE three

(SETTING: Beside the fountain, unbroken from before.)

(SERGIO sits beside DAGGETT.)

DAGGETT
(Watching the eels in the tank)
Oh hey, look, it's the actor, Sergio Pack. You're here to kill me, aren't you?

SERGIO
What? No. Of course not.

DAGGETT
No.
(Smiling from the eyes)
I've been saying that to everyone today. Last few weeks, people keep asking me for favors. "Mr. Daggett, um. I know you're incredibly busy, but." Kid, I'm just

about to drop, but I hear myself say, "Of course! How can I help?" Because it's my big night, I have to. But the next request is gonna finish me off.

SERGIO

(Sanctimonious)

The *Spyhole* says this week's celebrations at the Mountebank have been particularly debauched, even for you.

DAGGETT

Life's a party for artists like us. No, it is! What they don't say is, parties are hard work. All the goblins and trolls we have to pretend are people. It's criminal what they put us through, that's the truth.

(SERGIO thinks of the many hours he spends on the

couch, studying the shapes he can make with his fingers.)

But seriously, you're here to kill me, right?

SERGIO

W-w-

DAGGETT

For three years, I've been hovering on a rickety half-inch of plywood over a vat of venomous eels. I know I'm not just gonna walk out of here. It's Chekhovian law: something perturbs the surface of the water, it evokes a flavor of danger and fear—then bam! comes the payoff, when you least expect it.

SERGIO

That's . . . It's just your imagination.

DAGGETT

(Sighs)

Well, here's what I'm not imagining: Excuse my immodesty, but I'm this city's number one entertainment draw, and Randy Flynn can't afford to let me draw them somewhere else. But he hasn't offered me a contract extension, so I must conclude he has other plans for me. Sinister ones.

SERGIO

W-w-w . . . plans?

DAGGETT

Probably not though. I mean, who profits?
(Chuckling)
So much emotion this week. I can't believe it's all over. That's why I'm spooked this curtain's gonna be the final one.

SERGIO

"If it be not now, yet it will come. Readiness is all." Hamlet says that.

DAGGETT

Readiness for death, he means! Is that a thing? Listen, tell me this. What would you do if you knew you were about to die?

SERGIO

What?

DAGGETT

If, like Cinderella, you knew at the stroke of midnight you'd turn back into the loam from which you were formed. You know, die. What would you do?

SERGIO

I guess I haven't thought about it.

DAGGETT

(Smiling, with a hint of malice)
That's best. I think that's best.

will madden

SERGIO

. . .

DAGGETT

But seriously, say you knew it would all end at the stroke of twelve, and you had a show tonight. Would you go on? I mean, you're an actor. Brutal business, this. The things you had to do to make it, am I right?

   (SERGIO closes his eyes and watches NOODLE's
   head explode again.)

So would you? go on one last time? Could you imagine a better way to spend your last hours? After all, Hamlet's not just some bit part, it's the number one plum! Played by all the best actors as far back as Richard Burbage.

SERGIO

Burton. The one married to Elizabeth Taylor?

DAGGETT

They're divorced. Twice, actually. The question was, would you play Hamlet again?

SERGIO

I—

DAGGETT

All the choices you made to get here—not would you make them again, only an idiot—and, God knows it wasn't worth it, nothing is ever exactly *worth* it, but—did it give you any satisfaction, despite all the pain?

SERGIO

Y-y—. Geez, I don't know. I suppose so.

DAGGETT

Well decide.

rhadamanthus

(Insinuating)
You've only a few hours left to live.

SERGIO
W-w—.

DAGGETT
(Laughing)
The stage is the most deranged torture device ever constructed. People who say they love the theatrical life—the business they call show?—it's kind of a Stockholm syndrome. The monster who beats and berates you, oh it is gentle it is sweet it is wise. Shakespeare, for instance: only a man who hated the theater could have written Hamlet. To be or merely to seem. That's the play's real question. For a performer, what does it take to *be?* Talent, technique, presence? These things don't even begin. They are for, excuse me, for but playing at being. The suits and trappings of real substance.

SERGIO
(Confused, grasping at straws)
Is that what you're doing now? Wearing the trappings?

DAGGETT
When I sit in a restaurant, sometimes I see another performer across the room trying to act the part he plays on stage: the enormous personality, the booming voice, every word out of his mouth, God, so witty. Pathetic. It's pathetic. You feel like the only humane thing to do is offer your shoulder to cry on. "There, there, get it all out." 'Cause I know. 'Cause I've been that ludicrous ass in the restaurant, pretending to be Rico Daggett. Even in real life.
(Laughs and sighs.)
Crying is what I wanted to do. Every conversation I had, I felt like I was trying to entertain a particularly stupid child. Because that's the part they want us to play.

SERGIO

       (Stupidly)

Wait, a child?

DAGGETT

       (Smiles obscurely)

I started out as a choir boy at St. Ambrose's Church in New Guernsey. My only desire then was to share my gift with the world.

SERGIO

I believe it!

DAGGETT

Don't, it's bullshit. When I was eleven, I sang the solo in the offertory hymn, "Mors, Ubi Est Victoria Tua?" One Sunday morning, the congregation demanded an encore.

SERGIO

Did you?

DAGGETT

Church doesn't do goddamn encores!

       (Laughs)

Only, well, the ushers marched up, they took the holy gifts off the altar—the Body and Blood—and sent them 'round the back to do the processional over again. I don't know if you are religious, but . . . that's called "sacrilege." But what's the pastor gonna do, he cues the organ.

       (Leaning closer)

These people made God himself walk up the aisle twice so they could hear me again. That's why I'm a singer today.

rhadamanthus

SERGIO

Because of some heathens from New Guernsey?

DAGGETT

(With good humor)

The point is, as performers, that thirst for adoration is not merely our fatal flaw, it's our essential characteristic. Our patron saint.

SERGIO

(Shying away)

Mm. Perhaps I am an exception.

DAGGETT

(His jaw falling in mock surprise)

Ah, you're the one. At last I've found you!

SERGIO

For years, I avoided the stage altogether. I just studied performances I admired. I practiced them over and over in the mirror until I could duplicate every intonation, every look and gesture.

DAGGETT

Until your reflection shouted bravo!

SERGIO

What happened was, as I watched other actors, I started to see the ghost in the machine, as it were. Art pulling the strings of the body and voice. A doll with the face painted on.

DAGGETT

(As if clutching pearls)

Art's renowned imitation of life, you mean it's merely artifice?

SERGIO

(Earnestly)

Yeah! But the crowd, I noticed, they don't notice. They just laugh or applaud or cry like everything is real. I worried an audience would interfere with the development of my craft. That's why I restricted my performances to the mirror until I felt in complete command of my ability.

DAGGETT

(With irony)

You'd be the best judge, of course.

SERGIO

It was death for my career. In my social circles, I'd become the actor who didn't act. The quest for perfection had me completely paralyzed.

DAGGETT

See, that's why you're better motivated by a glorious piece of ass.

SERGIO

Then I thought, if only I could cheapen it somehow. Tear art down from the pedestal I'd placed it upon.

DAGGETT

Ah, so you just stopped giving a damn! Of course! I can really see it in your interpretation of Hamlet.

SERGIO

Well, no. I thought . . .

(Considers)

I thought if instead of auditioning, I won parts by doing favors for people, it would be the deeds I'd done upon the stage and not me. And that would free me from the mirror. Does that make sense?

rhadamanthus

DAGGETT

(Lowering his voice)

What favors did you do?

SERGIO

Have you ever been walking down the street and some busker is singing really, really beautifully, and you think: what's this con now, trying to get by on talent alone. Fuck him, that's not how the world works! There's an economy to these things.

DAGGETT

(Amused)

Without an agent and a promoter, the whole thing is obscene. Like jerking off in public. Go do that at home! Real art has an aura of hard dues paid.

SERGIO

Exactly! Ritual, blood sacrifice. Ooga booga! "Accept these our offerings!" To something invisible and maybe a little bit evil.

DAGGETT

Oh, a lot evil!

SERGIO

There's an affinity, I think, between art and crime. Thievery, forgery, propaganda, espionage, arson, homicide: these are an artist's true endeavors! They just happen to involve poetry, or paint, or song.

DAGGETT

Everyone's born a criminal. As children, we're creative at crime.

SERGIO

You don't really want art from someone the world hasn't corrupted with its stench.

DAGGETT

I've made a good living on that stench.

SERGIO

I believe it.

DAGGETT

Yeah, sniff. That hint to the cologne?

(DAGGETT bares his neck to SERGIO, who leans in, unthinking. He jerks back.)

SERGIO

(Soberly)

It's . . . It's Mara's blood, I think.

DAGGETT

(Unflinching, curious)

Are you sure?

SERGIO

Many people seem to be.

DAGGETT

Rumor is, you killed a man once.

SERGIO

(Quietly, as he studies the eels)

Accident. I can't remember doing it at all.

DAGGETT

Convenient, don't you think?

rhadamanthus

SERGIO

One second he had a face.

DAGGETT

(Nods)

To be, then not to be.

SERGIO

"What a piece of work is man. Like an angel in action. In apprehension like a god." When I say those lines, it's always that man's blast-open head I see.

DAGGETT

Interesting how that phrase enters English as an irony. "You're a real piece of work."

SERGIO

The play has got all the English in it. Not a creature was stirring, not even a mouse. Plagiarized from the first page.

DAGGETT

Now this—

(Produces a gun)

this is a piece of work.

(SERGIO recoils)

Beautiful, isn't it. Your fingers want to trace every line. Go ahead, touch it.

SERGIO

I'd prefer not.

DAGGETT

(With unnerving glee)

You wouldn't even feel it, I think, the bullet. Like your mother's breath in your hair, a whisper to wake you from a summer nap.

SERGIO

(Anxious)

I see no cause for this.

DAGGETT

I wonder what would happen if I fire this. Here, now. Not into the wall. I mean shoot somebody.

SERGIO

Are you—

DAGGETT

Seems impossible the show would still go on tonight, yet . . . I think they'd find a way. Tonight? Any other night, impossible, but tonight there's a chance.

SERGIO

(Backing away)

Quite, quite unlikely!

DAGGETT

I'd be curious to see. Chiefly curious. Could Flynn's fixers make this one disappear? I couldn't. Which is why I'm curious. Don't you ever wonder what's possible?

SERGIO

(Trying to remain calm)

Not often. No.

DAGGETT

Randall Flynn offered me a lot of money to shoot you before the show tonight. So when the curtain went up, there'd be blood on the water. Eels noshing in a frenzy.

(Makes a chomping sound with his teeth)

rhadamanthus

SERGIO

That's not true.

DAGGETT

Are you sure?

SERGIO
(Uncertain, loudly)

Yes!

DAGGETT

Why?

SERGIO
(Desperate)

He loves me like a son.

DAGGETT
(Laughs)

Does he?

SERGIO
(Unconvincing)

A very protective father.

DAGGETT

Only one bullet in this gun.
(Opens it and shows)
I sleep better knowing it's in the chamber. Under my pillow. It's like a promise. To myself, you know? One day, one day.

SERGIO

That's very, um.

DAGGETT

(Aims at SERGIO)

But now that I've shown you the gun, I've got to fire it.

SERGIO

T-t-that doesn't follow!

DAGGETT

Whose head would you put it in? The one bullet. Mine or yours, if you were me.

SERGIO

(On the verge of tears)

Nobody dies within the Mountebank Theater without permission! Not even by accident. That's the rules.

DAGGETT

See, what I was thinking: just this once, I *break* the rules. As if I had nothing to lose. Do I?

SERGIO

(Desperate, almost screaming)

Everything!

DAGGETT

(Just above a whisper)

What sort of person, I've cause to wonder, would kill a man who spared his life?

SERGIO

I'm sure I don't know.

rhadamanthus

DAGGETT

(Putting the gun away)

Do you consider this sparing yours?

SERGIO

(Regaining confidence)

It's not yours to spare.

DAGGETT

With Flynn, people never take the obvious out. Because if it looks easy, Flynn must have that escape covered. But how I see it, Flynn doesn't have everything covered. There is so very much he doesn't know.

SERGIO

I wouldn't take that chance.

DAGGETT

Flynn relies on your "wouldn't"s. Sure, he's a good reader of character. He can tell when you've got something you want to hide. But he's not supernatural. Wanna know the secret of Flynn's success? What created that aura of omniscience?

(Whispering)

Children. All that dirt he used to dig up and shout about in Krompachy Park. Secrets only the infernal judges could know. His informants were all kids. Whom no one saw, whom everyone ignored. They talked to Flynn and he listened. Then he made it all public in the town square. A lunatic with a funny accent, letting himself be laughed at. Until the truth of those crimes started to come out. Then people were afraid of him. They thought a ganglord must be protecting him, or he'd never have the guts to air the underworld's dirty laundry. Fact is, Flynn was just a punk whom somebody ought to have garroted a long time ago.

SERGIO

(Whispering)
Are you saying we could kill him?

DAGGETT

By now, he really can't be touched. But those early days, he was just too desperate to be afraid. Today he's got something to live for. Retribution is within his grasp.

SERGIO

Retribution for what?

DAGGETT

With Flynn it's hard to tell, isn't it? Which is the real him and which are the alter egos. The clue for me was: he's a fiend at breaking you down slowly, by millimeters so you don't realize it until you're there holding your own pieces. He knows how to do it because he's been broken.

SERGIO

By what?

DAGGETT

Right so, here's this man with his hooks in everything, who promises to act as Nemesis incarnate in this city. For every crime a punishment. A tit for every tat. In practice, however. You ever wonder why he picks on star crooners and—pardon me, facts—two-bit actors, but doesn't fry the real fish?

SERGIO

Because the tabloids love to revile entertainers?

DAGGETT

Because he used to be a performer. A man who lived for the stage. Who wanted it so bad, when he was out of work he stood in a public square and screamed of a Sunday afternoon. In costume. It's us he hurts because it's us he knows how.

SERGIO

Monty Bedlam, that old whore, he's having the time of his life. Doesn't care what happens so long as someone's there to watch. He'd tear out his own fingernails if he knew it'd draw a crowd.

DAGGETT

You're the big mystery of course. Nobody quite knows why Hamlet is supposed to be a hell for you.

SERGIO

I've earned this role as payment for the work I've done. Not in recompense for the sins I've committed.

DAGGETT

Because you aren't Hamlet at all. Even for a narcissist, you're far too simple.

SERGIO

Simple how?

DAGGETT

But your mother is queen of Big Botany. And like Gertrude, she remarried soon after her first husband died mysteriously, so there's that.

SERGIO

Are you saying something suspicious happened to my dad?

DAGGETT

Of course not. He simply went to bed one night and didn't wake up.

SERGIO

(Relieved)
That's what I thought!

DAGGETT

On account of the Polonius, most people think you killed some old man.
    (Pauses)
Death came on a-sudden for your grandfather, didn't it?

SERGIO

    (Squirming)
N-n-nooo, I'm sure he'd been lying there for hours.

DAGGETT

    (Smirking)
I watch your show imagining a thousand deaths for your granpop. Falls I like best. 'Cause of the way the corpse hits the stage and explodes under the stairs like a bag of wet trash.

SERGIO

I—

DAGGETT

Best part is: the head hammers straight down but the face breaks off to the side.

SERGIO

It's—

DAGGETT

Dodoville loves to see you suffer. It's hilarious when you're in pain! You grimace like termites are eating your stomach. You sweat like you got diarrhea. Your voice gets whiny and stuttering. Freckles appear on your face.

SERGIO

    (Grimacing, sweaty, freckly)
It w-w-was—

rhadamanthus

DAGGETT

Accidents, I know. Your whole life is accidents. Or is it? Maybe that night, you shot the man you meant to. Three people were in the room with you—

SERGIO

How do—

DAGGETT

Oh, don't you think I find out everything I can about those who get sentenced to the Mountebank? One was a buddy of yours, the second was loyal to your family, and the third? Some stranger you just met. You were frightened, you felt cornered. Suddenly your gun goes off and who gets killed? The one whose death would tax your conscience least.

SERGIO

I didn't, I didn't!

DAGGETT

I don't believe there is anything of an accident about you! You're not nearly as stupid as you pretend to be. You're careless and keep forgetting your disguise.

SERGIO

I just wanted to be in a play!

DAGGETT

Listen to you, the lies you tell yourself. Valorizing nepotism and cronyism to justify your career. If I just nod at your bullshit, you feel like a saint.

SERGIO

I'm not a—

DAGGETT

(Fiery)

What do you, at this moment, imagine yourself about to do tonight in this theater?

SERGIO

(Genuinely at a loss)

. . .

DAGGETT

I should have played Hamlet. Don't you think? And you should be the one out there mewling sappy, sentimental love songs. If the world were just.

SERGIO

Well—

DAGGETT

So here's the deal: I'm supposed to make Flynn a stack of cash tonight, and then you are supposed to make sure I never see my cut of it. So how's about neither of us give him much the satisfaction?

SERGIO

I'm not—

DAGGETT

Look, I don't want to die. And you, you think it's beneath you to kill a man on purpose. So how about the two of us skip town. Separately, I'd prefer, but if you feel you lack the agency to drive.

SERGIO

I can't leave. I've another three weeks left to this engagement.

DAGGETT

(Genuine laughter)

You'll murder me to act three more weeks in a play. In a role you're bad at! I'm beginning to think you have gumption after all. Listen, if you are going to do it, at least spare me the torment of the last show. That terrible song, those goddamn eels, me pretending I'm humbled-just-humbled by the outpouring

rhadamanthus

of love. Should I live another thousand years, I never want to feel an iota of human warmth again.

SERGIO

But Flynn said—

DAGGETT

And for fuck's sake, spare me the lifetime retrospective!

SERGIO

(Recklessly aggressive)
Why? Because your conscience is dirty?

DAGGETT

(Quiet a long moment)
Because I spent ten years in exile remembering. My memory is exhausted. One time up in the mountains, I got snowed in for four-five days. It terrified me, the tininess of that room. To make the universe bigger, I made a list of all the names I could put a face to, my entire life. It's my job to know people, so I could name quite a few. Eventually I reached all the way back to childhood. It's kinda funny, I thought maybe I shouldn't go back that far.

SERGIO

'Cause you weren't a star yet, right? What makes a person matter?

DAGGETT

Honest to God, it seemed like a sin to dredge them up. It's not that I know better people now, I don't. Andy Penult, he's the greatest jazz pianist who ever lived. An extension of the instrument, not the other way 'round. How many nights . . . Listen. After we made the arena crowds weep, it was off to the clubs. You gotta do that in this town, to butter the VIPs. No orchestra now, just Andy, Caboose, Tabby, Two-fish, maybe Buddy Cavalry gets called in. A crowd of, say, thirty. After that, no rest for the wicked, we play for an audience of just three-four in a little closet somewhere, these nights that go on till morning. For the journalists whose bullshit articles write you into legend. By now, just me and Andy on some out-of-tune upright. He's playing to the instrument's flaws, hammering the sour keys as much as he can. All the old songs about lovable imperfections bleed into one another like he doesn't even have to think. And maybe this butcher-show is the greatest thing on earth. These jerks came to hear Rico Daggett, but now they're listening to Andy Penult play the wrong notes on purpose. I gotta scramble to botch it just right alongside him. With dawn coming up, the piano sounds like a carnival winding down, you want to laugh and cry at once. These guys think my voice is angels shooting love right through 'em, but it's all Andy. All of it.

    (DAGGETT watches an eel leap momentarily out of
    the water)

Finally, the sun boils everybody's eyes out. Andy shuts the lid and turns right back into a goddamn block of wood. Drive a nail through his forehead, he wouldn't even blink. That's the kind of personality he has.

SERGIO
I read he has a quick wit.

DAGGETT
Believe what you want. Him and me had an emotional reunion this morning. I'm told it's been sixteen years. The press was there, keeping track! I said it felt like it could've been yesterday. Which was true: I never had a conversation with the guy the decade we worked together. Not even how's the soup. Fact is, I close my eyes now, I can't even picture his face.

SERGIO
Can you picture Mara's face?

    (DAGGETT pauses, weighing his options.)

rhadamanthus

DAGGETT

Anyways, I was snowed in up in the mountains, a couple cans of spam from starvation. I needed the memories for company, otherwise the end was too terrifying. I spent three goddamn hours thinking back to my childhood in New Guernsey, trying to remember the name of that ugly kid I used to cheat at marbles. No idea why it was important. Just if I didn't, I couldn't put it on the list. Thomas Pavlava. Platahava. Plavlahala. Let's call him Jerry. He lived two stories down in that dump of a building. Me, my mother, my two brothers . . . Jesus, I had two brothers once! Tommy-Jerry would meet me out in the courtyard. We chalked our circle on the walkway, behind a patch of impatiens. I hate impatiens, they're like flowers drawn by a three-year-old. Maybe they were violets. What matters is, Tommy used to pick his nose when he thought no one was looking. Listen, I hated marbles: playing them, counting them, stealing them. What I loved was watching Tommy pick his nose. He had these meaty fingers, dirt lines a half-centimeter thick under the nails. He really rummaged around, distending the nostril like he's got a shot put up there. Never even pulled anything out. Just liked the contours of dried booger inside his schnoz. So happy up in snotsville he lets me swipe his prize dobbert.

(His laugh almost a giggle)

If I could have any five minutes back, I'd watch Tommy P. pick his nose again.

SERGIO

And if you had two five minutes, would you spend the other saving or sparing Mara Carpenter?

DAGGETT

(Humming indistinctly at first, then in a forceful,
clownish voice)

I'll come back to Mara
if she comes not baaaack . . . to-o me.

Every fucking thing with you comes back to her, doesn't it?

    (The anger passes)

She comes back every night. That's what has me waking up in cold sweats: the ocean's not deep enough to keep her. Her hand rises out of the water alongside the boat. Then the head, those loose tresses tangled with seaweed. Creepy, but kinda beautiful at once.

                  SERGIO

What happens?

                  DAGGETT

    (With glee)

First thing, I smack her with an oar.

                  SERGIO

I wish that surprised me.

                  DAGGETT

To Mara and to Mara. I'm sick of all these Maras! Sometimes you just have to decide you're done with someone.

                  SERGIO

I know, it was really selfish of her to get murdered by you.

                  DAGGETT

If by miracle she was alive again in the next room, I wouldn't want to see her.

                  SERGIO

    (Righteous)

Because you'd have to face her judgment.

rhadamanthus

DAGGETT

(By now an expert at sidestepping these allegations)
I miss her. I do. Love her? Intensely. Maybe I never did. But murder Mara? Please. I don't mean I wouldn't take a human life. A dozen people I could name, dead in a blink if I could get away with it. Mara held me together. No, I wasn't faithful, I couldn't be. Those affairs were vital for our relationship.

SERGIO

Because you had to.

DAGGETT

Yes! Some women, I sing, they undress. Maybe they shuffle around a bit, touch their collar, and pretend they haven't made up their mind. Sometimes they want a little fight first. Maybe she says, "You murdered your wife, you disgust me!" So maybe I say, "But sweetheart, it just isn't true." She doesn't wanna hear that. She wants a confession. To feel like maybe I bumped off a famous actress to get to her.

SERGIO

Oh, fuck off.

DAGGETT

That's the best I can figure it anyways! Otherwise, what's the appeal? Look at me, Pack. I'm not as young as I used to be, and I was never handsome. My dick, you can see it if you like, it's short and knobby and curves to the right. I talk to them about grief and loneliness, shit nobody could ever believe. But they believe it. Soon, I do too. I've gotten myself so worked up, I need them, I'll die without them.

(Sighs)

Afterward, the illusion bursts. The same trick on myself, over and over. Each time I feel a little stupider for falling for it.

SERGIO

(Indignant)

So that's why you cheated on Mara? Because other women didn't satisfy you?

DAGGETT

(Slyly)

Do you know what sort of woman Mara Carpenter was? Before she could make her big break in Hollywood, she destroyed a wardrobe on the set of one of those sword and sandal pictures. A fit of old-fashioned loomy rage. Got sent back home to Sporqia for that.

SERGIO

I heard that was just a tabloid story.

DAGGETT

(Imitating Mara)

"Won't you please take those dirty things outside?": her most memorable line. Delivered with an earthy huff, so it's natural to misremember an "Oh." As in, "*Oh*, won't you please take those dirty things outside?" The things in question a trio of freshly lit cigars. The irony being Mara was not at all shy about taking a puff on a fat Cuban.

SERGIO

Are you implying something?

DAGGETT

Touring the world, I'd known more famous, more beautiful women, but Mara refused to sleep with me before we were married. I said I heard she'd never had scruples with other men. She told me I hadn't heard the half, but past did not dictate future, so love it or stuff it. But classy about it, you know?

rhadamanthus

SERGIO

(Earnest)

Elegance, always. That's what people remember.

DAGGETT

She'd brush me off, pleading pain or fatigue or—God knows what. Till she had me melting with sympathy. Only to act cavalier when I found her entangled with some other man that same night.

SERGIO

You're saying that's how she wooed you?

DAGGETT

It was really only her who enabled me to derive pleasure from other women. Without it, the tedium of my career would have destroyed me years ago.

SERGIO

This is too much!

DAGGETT

Traveling from town to town, telling the same stories to similar faces, going to bed with women I . . . You know, I've praised Hengebrook as the greatest town I've ever played so many times, I still have no idea if it's in Zahzia or Enderna.

SERGIO

Enderna.

DAGGETT

Swell, thanks. Our brawls became legendary. What got broken, who got called what. People started fabricating the details, like it was a privilege to witness one.

SERGIO

Are you saying it was embellishment when—

DAGGETT

Even I don't know what's true anymore. But it all came to a head once she felt her career had become no more than to stir up publicity for me.

SERGIO

That can't have been true.

DAGGETT

Fact is, there was nothing better for it. We wrote the setlist by light of the gossip column. Let them read Mara and me into fucking everything.

SERGIO

So you used her.

DAGGETT

Use. In this industry, it's what we do. She would have done the same. You said it yourself, talent is cheap. You do what it takes, and you learn not to apologize. There isn't even a point.

SERGIO

That's a rotten way to live.

DAGGETT

All the ways are rotten, kid.

SERGIO

Says you.

DAGGETT

Mara's was rotten. She would hurt herself to get at me. Threaten to drown herself just to give me grief.

rhadamanthus

SERGIO

Oh, here we go.

DAGGETT

I mean, what else did I keep her around for? She was no longer an actress, she said, she was my accessory.

SERGIO

Better story than killed by a giant jellyfish anyway. Too bad you didn't think of it thirteen years ago.

DAGGETT

(A glint in his eye)

After Mara died, people were disappointed I hadn't killed her. You could see it on their faces.

SERGIO

Yeah, you let everybody down.

DAGGETT

I'll say what I say, and you believe what you like, but murder was what they wanted. Fact. Let Rico do the unthinkable thing so they can run him out of town with fire and steel. What fun! That orgy of rage at the airport when I left, I memorized those faces. When I returned, I saw them again, the same ones but a hero's welcome.

SERGIO

Bullshit.

DAGGETT

This beast of a woman who pushed her way to the front, she wore the same dress on the tarmac. Both occasions, I'm sure of it. Probably because I'd helped her out of it once.

SERGIO

(Snorts)

You remember the outfit.

DAGGETT

Always remember the outfit. Let me explain something about women, Pack. When you meet her, observe how she dresses, how she carries herself, what sort of person she tries to come across as. Because it's the last thing on earth she really is. Try to seduce that woman, and you'll never get anywhere.

SERGIO

I happen to find—

DAGGETT

(Almost leering)

I'm telling you this because it's the same with men on stage: you have to train yourself to see who the performer is trying to hide.

SERGIO

W-w-what are you—

DAGGETT

(Glancing at his watch)

The man who calls himself Rhadamanthus, for instance. Listen to him for Christ's sake. He doesn't care about "economies of sin," he doesn't care about eradicating this city's wickedness. He's not even especially concerned with defeating his enemies and solidifying his control. The only thing he wants is to create a spectacle this city will never forget. The little foreign impresario is not his cover, it's his true face. And that's what makes him dangerous: he doesn't hate you, or me. He thinks of you as a prop, a piece of scenery in the drama he's staging before the whole city, with real lives for characters. And he wants a big finish. Actor kills crooner, crooner kills actor. One's as good as the other.

rhadamanthus

The death becomes the event, and the survivor—well, Flynn uses him in another show another day.

SERGIO

(Defensive)

I dunno why you keep saying—

DAGGETT

If you kill Rico Daggett tonight, you'll have to kill him again on the stage of the Mountebank every night for the rest of your life. But if you don't . . .

SERGIO

(Panicking)

I'll be the one who bleeds in tonight's tragedy. Help!

DAGGETT

Unless. We can refuse to give Flynn his big spectacle. The curtain opens on the final act and—what's this?—the chief protagonists are nowhere to be seen.

(Whispers)

There is a way out. That paranoid lunatic, Pierre Takoberu, always designed his madhouses with one more secret exit, just in case. It took me three years to find, but I know how to escape this theater. We two slip away, and no one hears from us again. Anticlimax. That's how to hurt him, that's the one punch he'll never recover from. Say the word and we break all the rules. Spit in the world's ever-gluttonous eye.

(Silence.)

SERGIO

But that's just the thing. I want to be on stage for the final act. I've lived my whole life to be in the big scene at the end.

will madden

DAGGETT
(Deflating, defeated)
God damn it, kid. Me too.

(They embrace.)

(CURTAIN)

ACT five
SCENE one

(SETTING: A catwalk above the eel tank at the Mountebank Theater.)

(AT RISE: FLYNN and HUMPHREY peer below, watching SERGIO and DAGGETT. HUMPHREY, without his glasses, fingers a dagger. FLYNN wears a pouch on his hip.)

HUMPHREY

Look at those two love birds.

FLYNN

Alas, poor Poppop. Did you know I costumed Polonius to remind Pack of his grandfather, whom he allowed to die alone at the bottom of the cellar stairs?

HUMPHREY
(His voice neutral)
Why'd he do that?

FLYNN
Unclear. Something about ducks or orangutans.

HUMPHREY
Sounds like Sergio.

FLYNN
How many times has Shakespeare compelled Pack to slap and spit on his grandfather in effigy, to taunt and degrade him, until he finally exterminates him like a pest in the wall?

HUMPHREY
I dunno, I never sat through the whole thing.

FLYNN
Night after night when Polonius' broken body is revealed, Pack sees himself as a child standing atop those stairs, too paralyzed to do anything but gawk.

HUMPHREY
(Turning toward FLYNN, as if it had just occurred to him)
You were offering him a chance to save Daggett, not to slay him.

FLYNN
(With a shrug)
But, of course, now he's squandered his one chance at redemption. How much greater his despair in an hour when he beholds Daggett murdered. Every scabbed-over wound gashed open anew!

rhadamanthus

HUMPHREY
(Almost bored, twirling the dagger)
Sinister.

FLYNN
Aha! But expedient for you! With Daggett using all his cunning to keep Pack at bay, he's not anticipating *your* dagger between his ribs. Finally, retribution for your sister's murder those many years ago!

HUMPHREY
After all I've done, this last thing should be easy.
(Gazing below)
This morning, he's called me his closest friend.

FLYNN
Bah. He once proclaimed his love to an oyster fork.

HUMPHREY
Whereas my only companion has been his wretchedness.

FLYNN
Don't forget your thirst for revenge.

HUMPHREY
His suffering comforts me. It lets me know there's beauty and worth in the choices I've made.

FLYNN
(Startled)
Stay focused. Clench the dagger in your fist. Heat the steel with your hatred, then put it to red-hot purpose!

HUMPHREY

When I look at him, I think: if he should live a hundred years, he might never experience a moment of happiness again.

FLYNN

(Tickled)

Luckily, he won't live a hundred minutes.

HUMPHREY

But what's more cruel than to leave him in his agony?

FLYNN

Murdering him, of course! Consuming his flesh in an unholy sacrament!

HUMPHREY

Is that revenge, though? or mercy?

FLYNN

Who cares, so long as it's bloody!

HUMPHREY

I care! I'm the one who has purchased his life through their suffering. Look at the man I've become. A hired thug. I've killed people. I've betrayed friends.

FLYNN

All for nothing if you don't act now.

HUMPHREY

I know my part in this. Better than anyone.

FLYNN

Then why do you miss your cue? You have until the curtain falls on Daggett tonight before your contract on his life expires.

rhadamanthus

HUMPHREY

I remember the terms.

FLYNN

Then go at it, man! The moment is ripe.

HUMPHREY

(He holds the dagger in both hands, the blade facing down. With head bowed and eyes closed, he murmurs something inaudible. When he lifts his head again, his eyes are suddenly clearer.)

But is his death what I really want?

FLYNN

Tsk. Weakness. Out of character for Philip Humphrey.

HUMPHREY

(Defiant)

Sir, what do you know of him?

FLYNN

Enough. I know what he's inflicted upon himself in service of this vendetta. Three years toiling at the beck of his enemy, watching Daggett insult the memory of one dear to him. Too much for any man to stand.

HUMPHREY

(Darkly)

I'll stand what any can and more.

FLYNN

Stand it no longer! Instead, step out at last upon the stage of your revenge.

HUMPHREY

You want to sensationalize his murder as a publicity event for your theater. But his life is mine and mine alone!

FLYNN

Why so defensive? This is what you've worked for. Will you let the fruit of your labor rot in the field? No. Take the scythe and reap your due!
> (He tries to join hands with HUMPHREY around the dagger, but HUMPHREY pulls away.)

Are you worried Dodoville will never know why Rico Daggett was slain, to sate the fury of Mara Carpenter? Because I can guarantee that for you.

HUMPHREY

How?

FLYNN

We'll make a show of it! When Daggett mounts the platform to sing tonight, you'll sneak on behind him. He'll hear the rotting wood creak—feel it adjust to your weight—and know what you've come to do. But too afraid of losing balance and tumbling into the tank, he won't even turn his head. Instead, he will kneel as he always does and reach out for some invisible hand to steady him. It won't come. As the winch lifts you both, he will feel himself falling fully into your power. For tonight, it's your presence that will command the stage.
> (FLYNN reaches into the pouch on his hip.)

Which means, of course, you'll be in costume.
> (He pulls out a mask and gossamer robe. The mask is the face of a sea monster with tentacles about the scalp.)

HUMPHREY

(Scoffing)
"Giant Jellyfish Returns For Blood." Is that your angle?

rhadamanthus

FLYNN

The audience will be your mirror: as Daggett reads your intent on their faces, you will see his terror. The music will swell and crash, cuing him to perform. Conditioned by fear, he'll lift his voice in song as he always does, exposing his throat to your knife. With death approaching, the melody will cramp and quaver upon his lips.

(His face lights up in a kind of ecstasy.)

His rendition tonight will be just for you. "Come back, Mara, come back." Teach him, then, what returns from the crevasse. Just as his voice hits its peak, just before the divine note begins its plunge back to the mortal realm, slash his windpipe and throw him into the tank. I've directed the orchestra to fall quiet. How quiet it'll be. The audience will watch the foam on the water as Daggett succumbs to the frenzy of countless churning sea monsters.

HUMPHREY

(Scoffing)

A school of fish holding the scales of justice. Your most absurd spectacle yet.

FLYNN

(With a smirk)

Wait, yet! Once the shock has passed, remove the mask and show your face.

HUMPHREY

Who am I? An unknown.

FLYNN

You and your sister bear a strong resemblance. With hair and makeup done up like hers, people will say it was Mara herself.

HUMPHREY

(Glumly)

Nobody would ever know me for Mara Carpenter.

FLYNN

Nonsense!
>(Puts a wig on HUMPHREY's head and holds up a photo for comparison)

Anyone who didn't know better would say this is the *same person,* only thirteen years older.
>(Chuckling)

The poetry of it! After years of singing for her return, Mara comes back at last. For blood!

HUMPHREY

I've lived my whole life in her shadow. Even as a child, her persona upon the stage swallowed me whole. I've no desire to give Mara what Philip has long-labored and suffered for!

FLYNN

Give her nothing! Do you think no inquiries will be made? As to who killed Rico Daggett at the apex of his fame? The truth will come out! People will learn who and what you are.
>(HUMPHREY freezes, the face draining of color)

What have I said?

HUMPHREY
>(On the verge of tears)

No inquiry was ever made for Mara. One day she was gone and nobody bothered to find out why! They just wrote her off and said oh well. After all those professions of love. After all she . . .

FLYNN

Even more reason to do this! Show the absentee umpires of the law how to keep score. You—not them—had the righteousness to seize the cur by the throat and administer justice.

rhadamanthus

HUMPHREY

(Angry)

What do you know of justice, tyrant?

FLYNN

(Laughing)

And think of what it'll do for your reputation. Move over Rico Daggett. From this day forth, you will be the Mountebank's most celebrated entertainer!

HUMPHREY

(Disparaging)

My infamous cameo.

FLYNN

Not at all. Any show you like! With Daggett gone, this theater will need a new star. At last, you'll have the career you've always wanted.

HUMPHREY

(Hesitant)

I've worked here a long time. I know what it means to be one of your performers.

FLYNN

What worse could you endure than the countless little cuts Daggett inflicts upon you daily? The indignity like an itch begging to be scratched. Do it then. Take the satisfaction that is rightfully yours. I am the law in this theater. I sanction this action!

HUMPHREY

(Quietly)

In my ledger, that man has accrued such a debt to me, the balance could never be repaid by any one action. Only by holding him fast at the precipice of death, making him tremble at the imminent judgment of God, succumbing to a thousand frightful failures of courage until at last his heart is stretched so tight as to tear—that alone I could stomach to call justice!

FLYNN
(Frustrated)
Don't forget you have your own crimes now, your own infernal sentence to be handed down! Fail me in this, and I will make you repeat your cowardice upon this stage for as long as you draw breath.

HUMPHREY
I have paid you in advance through blood service! By what abortion of accounting do you attempt to collect on both ends?

FLYNN
I am Rhadamanthus. What's mine is mine. But what is hell's, I'm also licensed to claim.

HUMPHREY
That's just a story made up by some imbecile at the newspaper. I'll never debase myself in one of your shame shows.

FLYNN
The lines are written, the parts have been cast!
(Retrieves a scroll from his pouch)
About a hitman who trails a quarry for years only to let him get away at the end. A role for you. No one else could play it so convincing! I call it *The Slippery Eel*.

HUMPHREY
I refuse.

rhadamanthus

FLYNN

I brought Daggett back to Dodoville for you. Scoured the earth so you could satisfy the blood honor of your whore of a sister.

HUMPHREY

(Shaking with emotion)

Paid in full.

FLYNN

Your duty is not. Daggett's death at your hand is prescribed by your family honor. Or will you violate the law of your own blood?

HUMPHREY

Excuse me, but what do you know of me or mine?

FLYNN

Everything. Name it! I know about their education, political allegiances, employment history. I even know the secret ingredient in your mother's guava chutney.

HUMPHREY

All that might be written in the ledger for a judge of heaven or hell. But Randall, there is so very much you do not know.

FLYNN

(Snarling)

Try me.

(HUMPHREY hesitates.)

This town's perverse need to prove away my omniscience. Where does it come from? I challenge you then. Name one fact I'm not privy to. One I could give a shit about!

will madden

HUMPHREY

That won't work. I'll give nothing away.

FLYNN

(With a superior bellow)

But you've nothing to give! I have all I need, and the rest is trivia.

HUMPHREY

You wish.

FLYNN

Sometimes I do!

HUMPHREY

The whole spectacle on which your empire relies is shrouded in a lie. And it can be exposed with a single light of truth.

FLYNN

It cannot.

HUMPHREY

The truth that Rico Daggett never killed Mara Carpenter.

FLYNN

A lie!

(Smiling faintly)

Or, what is about the same, a truth that cannot be proved.

HUMPHREY

Can.

FLYNN

(Reprovingly)

And certainly not by you.

rhadamanthus

HUMPHREY

Who better than I? For I am she!

(Holding up the photo for comparison)

The oft-bewailed woman who got pitched overboard by that infamous drunk when they came to blows over who would shoot first at shuffleboard.

FLYNN

(Without inflection)

Wait, come again.

HUMPHREY

Who watched him stand at the railing with tears in his eyes as her clothes dragged her to the murky depths. I called out to Ricky for help—Help, I said!—but he just watched me, flailing his arms uselessly, as the boat's motor carried him away.

FLYNN

(Whimsically)

So the sea monster actually saved you, is that it? Poor creature, so much maligned!

HUMPHREY

I managed to cling to a cooler full of Wild Berry Fanta I had thrown at him earlier.

FLYNN

Why didn't he cut the engine and pick you up?

HUMPHREY

I was the only one who could operate the boat.

FLYNN

Then why didn't you explain it to him?

HUMPHREY

We were both incredibly drunk. Why else fight over shuffleboard?

FLYNN

It's almost more amazing that he made it back to land than you did.

HUMPHREY

Eight days and nights at sea, baking in the sun or freezing in the ocean spray, I prayed for rescue, surviving on Fanta until the seawater started to look tempting . . .

FLYNN

(Looking around for someone to appeal to)

Really, this?

HUMPHREY

I only learned from the trawler captain who found me why no search effort had been made. On account Ricky had said he witnessed me eaten alive by a fucking jellyfish!

FLYNN

A squid, at least, would have lent this affair some dignity.

HUMPHREY

Because he was afraid no one would ever want to sleep with a man too coward to rescue a woman from a tranquil sea.

FLYNN

(Rubbing his temples)

Anyways, I confess I did not know about the shuffleboard. But the salient point: I was certain Philip Humphrey was never real.

rhadamanthus

HUMPHREY

Who's not real? I've never left your side.

FLYNN

A famous actress might have a talentless brother who was born anywhere in the world. But a twin? It was easy to check the birth records at St. Agnew's Hospital. That was your mistake.

HUMPHREY

Now do you want to hear yours?

FLYNN

Absolutely.

HUMPHREY

That he was talentless. Mara embodied Dodoville's beauty and spirit, but it was Philip who had the real gift.

FLYNN

(Astonished)
For acting?! You're the first to think that.

HUMPHREY

But I won't be the last! As Mara, I had to make unsavory compromises just to earn my way in this town. But as Philip, I infiltrated Dodoville's deadliest gangs and bent them to my will. Now this city is mine to allot whatever fate I choose for it. *I* shall be its Rhadamanthus!

FLYNN

No, Mara.

HUMPHREY

Leave Mara her watery grave. The crowd may have been enchanted by how she swayed her hips and gave face, but it's as Philip Humphrey that I confound even the infallible reader of souls.

FLYNN

I've always known who you are.

HUMPHREY

But do you know what I am?

FLYNN

Surely.

HUMPHREY

Do you? A stage actor stands before an audience who's already willing to be gulled by craft. But if I successfully plied my skills on someone whose fortune depended on his ability both to *seem* and *be* un-gullible . . .

FLYNN

Intriguing.

HUMPHREY

It's almost necessarily true, isn't it? That the world's greatest actor is unknown, because nobody has ever realized he's acting.

FLYNN
(Sourly, glancing at his watch)
All right, I have the gist now. You may skip to where you intend to kill me.

HUMPHREY
(Off-guard)
I prepared a whole speech.

rhadamanthus

FLYNN

Of course you did. But this reversal is pointless. Grant that you have deceived me: over the years, you have nevertheless been my finest, most perfect instrument. With you in hand, I have crushed my most formidable enemies, I have climbed to this city's apex of power. Even should you manage to overthrew me now, who you've been and what you've seemed to be has not differed in the least: namely, the executor of my will. The betrayal you commit in this moment is not against me but all the suffering you have already endured.

HUMPHREY

(Defiant, weeping)

I am greater than my pain!

FLYNN

Enough. My sincere advice is to keep to the path you've been traveling. Otherwise, you will only have wasted a decade of toil.

HUMPHREY

Not wasted. Before I kill you, you should know your death is the final move in a game you lost long ago. The roots of your organization are black with mold and decay. Your empire is hollow. A blight has infested its living pulp, and although the branches still bear leaves, the trunk is already dead.

FLYNN

Ah. You are referring to the cohort of the Department's grad students ready to invade at your signal, am I right? Just as well that I've posted my ushers to be ready for them.

(HUMPHREY's face registers the danger. FLYNN looks at her with sympathy.)

Give up, Mara. Do as I ask, and we'll overlook this indiscretion.

HUMPHREY

Your men are outnumbered and I am the more skilled assassin. You have no recourse.

FLYNN

(Glancing around)

So this is checkmate then? Very good. So, let's have an end. Stab!

(FLYNN straightens, exposing his torso)

HUMPHREY

(Flummoxed)

You're not gonna . . .

FLYNN

It's poor gamesmanship to delay the inevitable. Timely now, it's the only move you've left yourself. Ha!

(HUMPHREY hesitates. FLYNN sprays something snatched from his bag into her eyes. They grapple. HUMPHREY is stabbed and pushed over the edge of the catwalk. FLYNN struggles to regain his breath as he gazes over the railing.)

God damn it, he missed the tank!

(BLACKOUT)

SCENE two

(SETTING: Before the tank of eels on stage of the Mountebank. Mt Myrtle, the volcano in the background, has deepened in color and grown in brightness.)

(AT RISE: SERGIO and DAGGETT face the audience together.)

SERGIO
On the River Dodos, the flow of justice has been dammed

DAGGETT
By men who say "Damn the law"

SERGIO
Crime courses the streets like sewage

will madden

                    DAGGETT

Offending heaven with its stench

                    SERGIO

           (Indicating with his arms)

This theater is precinct to one called Rhadamanthus

                    DAGGETT

Lord of Hades and Infernal Judge

                    SERGIO

Who holds court here in hell on Earth

                    DAGGETT

Condemning the wicked to repeat their sins

                    SERGIO

In perpetuum

                    DAGGETT

Ad nauseum

                    SERGIO

Making a spectacle of their pain and suffering

                    DAGGETT

Which he exploits for prestige and power

                    SERGIO

While this reckoning makes our city's failures fouler

                    DAGGETT

By unlawful punishment, our lives grow more lawless

rhadamanthus

(As the volcano begins to shake, animals can be heard to screech in terror.)

SERGIO
(Still in darkness, pantomiming a gorilla)

From apes we came, to apes we return.

DAGGETT

Every morsel won with violence

SERGIO

Each procreation an act of rage

DAGGETT

Our speech reduced to howls and bleating

SERGIO

We labor with flint and bone

DAGGETT

Making worship with froth and blood

SERGIO

Pounding our feet

DAGGETT

To the pounding in our breast

BOTH
(Striking their chests and shouting)

Boom boom!

SERGIO

Blood of our enemies

                    DAGGETT
           (Raking his nails down his face)
Our costume and mask

                    SERGIO
Blood of our veins

                    DAGGETT
           (Arms crossed like a corpse)
Our burial shroud

                    SERGIO
           (Turning toward DAGGETT)
Is this our fate?

                    DAGGETT
Inevitable!

                    SERGIO
Inexorable!

                     BOTH
Boom boom!

           (SERGIO and DAGGETT kneel and worship the
           volcano. For some reason, wind blows inside the theater.)

                    SERGIO
Stony strength of the mountain

                    DAGGETT
Cleanse this land with fire and ash

rhadamanthus

SERGIO

With brimstone crush untoward ambition

DAGGETT

In blackest smoke smother greed

SERGIO

Wither hypocrisy in scalding steam

DAGGETT

Roast licentiousness in sulfuric flame

SERGIO

Only you have the might to scour away iniquity

DAGGETT

Only your righteousness can torch out decay

SERGIO

With fire and ash

DAGGETT

With ash and fire

BOTH

Boom boom!

SERGIO

We cry out for justice.

DAGGETT

To the bowels of the earth, we cry

SERGIO

For justice!

DAGGETT

For justice!

BOTH

Boom boom!

(The volcano smokes and fulminates. Orange light erupts from the cone.)

DAGGETT
(Shrinking as if scalded)

A-ye!

(The lighting returns to as before. Silence hangs. SERGIO and DAGGETT exchange embarrassed looks about what just came over them.)

(Enter PARLIAMENT in disguise, leading a BOTANIST ARMY in courier uniforms, each holding a potted palm tree in front of their faces as camouflage. They sway lightly from side to side.)

SERGIO

Seriously?

GOON 1
(As BOTANIST, accent unplaceable)
Harro, ve are heeyuh wid ze palum trees for ze luau sheen?

rhadamanthus

PARLIAMENT
(Putting down her plant, she runs to SERGIO and removes her mustache)
Mr. Pack. Quickly, step away from that man.
(Pulls him away from DAGGETT)

DAGGETT
Have I swallowed a bomb?

SERGIO
(Anxious, remembering their last meeting)
Billie Parliament. What are you doing here?

PARLIAMENT
I came as emissary from your parents, Mr. Pack. I'm here to pull you out.

SERGIO
Of?

PARLIAMENT
No fear. You no longer need to maintain your cover.

SERGIO
(Shiftily)
Ah, my cover.

PARLIAMENT
I asked to be sent in repayment for you saving my life those years ago. Your courage in that frightful situation made me a sympathizer with the Department.

SERGIO
I—How kind of you to remember.

PARLIAMENT

Please, it's dangerous to stand so close to the corpse.

(Leads SERGIO further away from DAGGETT)

After our nation's humiliating defeat in the Zahzian War, Randal Flynn ascended to ganglord on the fervor for retribution. But now reconstruction funds flow in from America and the economy is recovering. People are putting away their former rancor to welcome the fruits of prosperity.

SERGIO

Money salves every wound!

PARLIAMENT

Aye. And science shows the way forward. The U Dodo Department of Botany, chaired by your very educated mother, is the only crime organization that can carry our city into a future of enlightenment.

DAGGETT

Pardon me, about this bomb I've swallowed.

PARLIAMENT

(Whispering)

Mr. Pack, our contacts have uncovered a plot within Flynn's organization to frame Mr. Daggett's murder on you, thus legitimizing you as a target in the upcoming gang war.

SERGIO

Your contacts?

DAGGETT

Wait. *Frame* him? Then he's not my assassin? Ye gods, I just wasted my last hour on that imbecile!

rhadamanthus

PARLIAMENT

Excuse me.

(Moving between DAGGETT and SERGIO)

I must ask the corpse to stand a non-incriminating distance from Mr. Pack.

(Turning to SERGIO)

Sir, the Department has been monitoring you carefully ever since you became a mole within the Flynn organization.

SERGIO

M——. Monitoring me through whom?

(HUMPHREY falls from the catwalk, landing in front of the fountain. Sitting up feebly, he puts on newly-broken glasses.)

FLYNN

(Above)

God damn it, he missed the tank!

PARLIAMENT

Oh dear.

DAGGETT

(Aside)

Is this good for me, I wonder?

HUMPHREY

(Sprawled out)

O the muses, I'm undone!

DAGGETT

You weren't supposed to fall on my head, by any chance?

HUMPHREY
(Gesturing weakly toward the palm trees)
Can it be? Have I died and gone to paradise?

DAGGETT
No, they're potted. You are still at the Mountebank.

SERGIO
(Attending HUMPHREY)
What's this, blood? My God, you're wounded!

DAGGETT
(Also attending)
Oh, my poor Humphrey! Do you suppose you might have just died fighting off my killer?

PARLIAMENT
(To SERGIO)
Mr. Pack, I must insist you maintain a distance between yourself and Mr. Daggett's body.

DAGGETT
I'm still using it, fool!

HUMPHREY
(Coughing up blood)
For deception my mother conceived me. Under a dissembling star was I born! Too long now has Dodoville reaped the fruit of my treachery.

DAGGETT
(Holding HUMPHREY's hand)
Oh, my sweet valet, you're delirious, I don't understand a word. Hush, it won't be long now.

rhadamanthus

PARLIAMENT
(Pulling SERGIO aside)
Mr. Pack, I have news for you. Your mother has announced her intention to retire as Department Chair in two years. And she has named you as her successor!

(HUMPHREY groans at the news)

SERGIO
Me? I've never cracked a science book in my life.

PARLIAMENT
You shall have two years to surfeit yourself in the Garden Father's secrets. After that, it will fall on you to rule the city!

DAGGETT
(Aside)
Jesus. I was almost ready to give maniacal botany a shot.

HUMPHREY
(To DAGGETT)
Before I die, sir, there's something I want to tell you.

DAGGETT
Hush now, I know. I know Mara was your sister. Do you think she never spoke of her twin, how one day he hoped to be an actor too? I felt sorry for you. You clearly never had the . . . You know, the talent.

(HUMPHREY stiffens and chokes)

PARLIAMENT
Wait a tick. Is this the young lady who threatened to kill me when I was president of the loomy union? Whose side is she on?

DAGGETT

What ho! A lady?

PARLIAMENT

Mein Gott, it's true what they say. They fall from the sky into your lap, yet you scarcely notice them.

DAGGETT

Who, Humphrey?

(Searches her)

Son of a! My Philip's a filly. I always thought you had a feminine touch.

(HUMPHREY chokes and writhes)

PARLIAMENT

(To SERGIO)

I've witnessed scores of people killed in union disputes. This is by far the least believable death rattle I have ever seen.

(To HUMPHREY, loudly as if she's deaf)

You didn't really hope to be an actress, did you, sweetheart?

DAGGETT

(Sitting beside HUMPHREY, tears in his eyes)

I meant what I said before. I wouldn't have blamed you if you avenged your sister. It would have put a nice symmetry on things: me dying on account of Mara, as she died on account of me. Only, I really did hope you'd hold my hand. Just as I'm doing now for you. As gloomy as it sounds, you are the only thing like a friend I've known since we lost Mara at sea.

SERGIO

(To PARLIAMENT)

Are they really gonna make me Department Chair?

rhadamanthus

HUMPHREY

(To DAGGETT, dying)

Lean closer, please. Hear this.

DAGGETT

Save your strength, darling, it's all right. I would have liked to warm the sheets with you too, if I'd known. I dreamed about it a couple times anyways, as is.

SERGIO

(To PARLIAMENT)

He must've fallen forty feet onto that knife. How is he still talking?

PARLIAMENT

(To SERGIO, shrugging)

Sometimes it really does take hours.

HUMPHREY

(Groaning)

All the world's a theater, and everyone a willing dupe. For years I have donned this simple costume and you have trusted it before your own senses.

(Removing glasses)

See me now for who I truly am.

FLYNN

What the hell? You look exactly the same.

HUMPHREY

(Grunting and breathing belaboredly)

I'm sorry, Ricky. It was me who had Flynn bring you back. To Dodoville. So I could watch you be afraid for your life on stage every night. To wail and suffer for everyone to see. I made sure you never missed a show.

DAGGETT

Wait, *you* brought me here? All this shit was on your account?

SERGIO

Whoa! Seriously, Philip? That was really dick.

DAGGETT

That soulless snake, Flynn, I could understand. But you?

FLYNN

(Above)

It's true, Daggett.

DAGGETT

I could have lived out my days in peace and quiet—in the shadow of a majestic snow-capped mountain instead of a fucking volcano!—but you dragged me back to this city, back under these terrible lights, and had me sing that God-awful song. Just to watch me shit my pants over those eels!

FLYNN

(Climbing down a steel ladder)

The eels were her idea. The perfect way to make you relive your terror upon the water, night after rickety, sea-tossed night.

DAGGETT

(Enraged)

God damn you to those Goddamn eels!

(Tries to drag HUMPHREY into the tank)

HUMPHREY

Ow ow ow.

rhadamanthus

DAGGETT

You're not getting out of this by being heavy.

> (Rolls up up a sleeve, storms over to the fountain to retrieve a live eel from the water)

HUMPHREY

No. What are you doing!

FLYNN

> (Alarmed)

Fool! It's too dangerous!

DAGGETT

> (Fishing)

Dangerous, nothing. Come 'ere, slippery!

> (Aside)

New Guernsey guddling champion, 1957, me!

> (Catches one)

Just deserts. Eat up!

> (Force-feeds the eel to HUMPHREY, who chokes wetly, shudders, dies.)

> (Silence falls.)

FLYNN

Idiot. The eel has now poisoned you too.

PARLIAMENT

> (Pushing SERGIO aside)

Please, Mr. Pack. As of now, it is the utmost necessity.

FLYNN

You are lost.

(Somberly)

Although it must come as some comfort that at the very end you are finally vindicated.

DAGGETT

What do you mean?

FLYNN

Only that now it will be shown you did not murder Mara Carpenter thirteen years ago. On account you did so just now.

DAGGETT

No, but this is . . .

FLYNN

(Smiling wickedly.)

Check the body. Surely there is some . . . distinguishing mark she acquired over your years of acquaintance.

(DAGGETT's fingers explore the corpse. Suddenly, he recoils, his feet pushing him away across the floor. Then he draws close again on his hands, collapsing upon the body)

DAGGETT

(Roaring theatrically)

Alas, my life, my light! I fled to the corners of the earth from my cowardice and shame, but it was your love that found me and brought me back. Darling, how many times have I prayed to see your face again, only to learn that my prayer was being answered every day, every hour!

(Breathing hard)

rhadamanthus

O God, my side hurts. It's like an avalanche, all I've said and done to you these last years, every pebble of cruelty and spite, crashing down like a mountain of regret. Is it the poison making my breath so shallow? Is this the end already? I can almost see that distant shore.

    (Sings)

> *Come back my darling Mara*
> *Come back from the sea*
> *I'll go back to Mara*
> *If she comes not back—*

SERGIO

W-wait, shaddap! An antidote is writ
In learned texts of Departmental power:
It's purple, fragrant, small—a hardy flower
That blooms upon the bed of cinder spit
   from Myrtle's magmic peak. Its occult wealth:
   Distilled in petals' silken crucible
   Sulfuric mites will prove reducible
   To dewy beads of mercury's most health-
some milk. The potent serum thus extruded
Is strong to neutralize contaminants.
Just drip upon the tongue—or slather it
Like ursine lard across the breast denuded.
   So long it's fauna-based that's plaguing us,
   Results are almost instantaneous!

PARLIAMENT

    (Beaming with pride)

Most scientifically put, Mister—Or should I say, Doctor Pack?

DAGGETT

(Choking as the poison takes effect, seeing the horrors of hell behind his eyes)

Flynn. Surely you have some of this magic bloom-dew on hand!

FLYNN

(Darkly)

It's in the theater somewhere. You have twenty minutes before paralysis sets in. Taste everything.

DAGGETT

(Producing the gun from his pocket)

Or I'll kill you. I'll take you with me.

FLYNN

That is your prerogative. But time is short. Don't you have a smarter move?

DAGGETT

(Places gun to FLYNN's forehead)

I'm afraid it's a narrative necessity.

FLYNN

(Executes a disarming maneuver and points the gun at DAGGETT)

Just an aesthetic preference.

DAGGETT

(Grimacing as the pain worsens)

Shoot me. Please. Spare me the toxin's effect.

FLYNN

(His mouth hardening)

You may go. Seek the Lady Myrtle's succor for your salvation.

rhadamanthus

DAGGETT
(Sobbing, shouting)
A thousand hells be-wretch your heart!
(Takes car keys from HUMPHREY's pocket and exits)

(Offstage: sounds of an engine turning over, then tires pulling away with a screech)

FLYNN
(Brandishing the gun)
Everyone holding a palm tree: your coup is thwarted. Get the fuck out of my theater.

(BOTANISTS glance uncertainly between each other.)

SAMSON
(Offstage)
Wait!
(Enters, dressed shabbily like SERGIO PACK, wielding a machete.)

PARLIAMENT
Two of you?

SAMSON
Oi, this is *my* fashion statement!
(Staggers toward FLYNN with sloppy swipes of the blade)
Flynn, you parasitic moss! You robbed me of my hereditary rights. But tonight I reestablish myself as ganglord. Tonight I restore underworld supremacy to *legitimate* Loogeys.

FLYNN
Go home, Sammy. You're drunk.

SAMSON

No. This ends tonight. The Department has recognized my claim to the Siding. By this hand I uproot thee. With this machete, I hack away—

FLYNN

(Shoots SAMSON, the report deafening)

I suppose some things are necessary after all.

(As SAMSON slips in HUMPHREY's blood, FLYNN pushes SAMSON's body into the eel tank. Splashing and screaming continue while FLYNN gives dirty looks to BOTANISTS in courier uniforms.)

GOON 1

(As BOTANIST, to the other BOTANISTS)

Courage! The seed that dies in earth is born again!

GOON 2

(As BOTANIST)

A demon name has Rhadamanthus, but he bleeds like a man. Draw forth and lay in!

(BOTANISTS each grab a knot on their potted trees and pull. Nothing happens.)

FLYNN

O forest that walks! Inside your bark, your usurping daggers are glued fast within their sheaths. Or did you think none would betray your plot to me?

GOON 1

We've fists enough yet.

rhadamanthus

GOON 2

Aye, and teeth.

FLYNN
(Shouting)

I've a round of bullets, motherfuckers! If I die, I die barrel-hot! How many of you came ready to make their final charge today?

(BOTANISTS lay down pots and exit.)

(SAMSON's screaming continues.)

PARLIAMENT

Come, Mr. Pack. Your parents are waiting for you. The Department shall press its advantage after Flynn's raises the curtain on an empty stage tonight.
>(She strikes a pose at center stage, raising her fist triumphantly.)

This tyrannical age of art and poetry is doomed. Long live the dictatorship of science!

(PARLIAMENT and SERGIO exit, leaving the stage empty except for FLYNN.)

FLYNN
(To himself)

He feared nothing on earth so much as those eels! He called them "banana wrappers" because peels rhymed with eels! How the fuck could I know he'd stick his hand in there?
>(Covering his face)

I spent my life building this theater, for this moment, and now I've no fucking finale!

(He places the muzzle of the gun under his chin, closing his eyes. Slowly, grimacing, he pulls the trigger. The gun, chamber empty, clinks impotently. FLYNN's eyes reopen. He looks around, as if seeing the theater for the first time. His face takes on a defiant edge.)

Ted Hornet! Victoria Schmutz!

(Enter VICTORIA in costume for her one-woman show, *How I Replaced Ginger Adams as Host of Inspiring People*, carrying the bloody head of Ginger Adams.)

(Re-enter HORNET, shyly, in a palm tree courier's uniform)

Get a photography team in here. Document every spot of gore, every thwarted weapon. Time to rewrite tonight's debacle into the most celebrated event in our city's history. Another unforgettable occurrence upon the stage of Dodoville's mythic Mountebank Theater!

(To audience)

When overt fact obstructs the path to glory
'Tis meet to pay some stooge to spin the story

(FLYNN exits with VICTORIA. HORNET, briefly undecided, follows.)

(Palm trees remain alone on stage. Like, ominously, or whatever.)

(SAMSON's screaming continues.)

(CURTAIN)

EPILOGUE

(Enter NOODLE as a ghost, wearing FLYNN's sea-creature costume. He waits for SAMSON's screaming to stop. Several comic false finishes.)

                    NOODLE
(Voice echoing with digital reverberation behind the mask)
Vindicta mihi! At last, it is accomplished!
        (Removes mask, revealing parts of his head still missing. His voice normalizes.)
After I got the porridge got blown outta my skull those years ago, my soul absconced to hell where I met this guy sitting on a big stone chair. Elfin little fella with bull's horns on his forehead. Waaaay too heavy for him, you know? Said he was called Rhadamanthus—and that's his proper name too, him regretting the confusion. Used to rule Crete three thousand years ago. Now he judges the damned on account of his rep for, ya know, arbitrariness. For me, he says, hell it must be, 'cause I killed all those folks for money. Also, if we're

honest, oft in ways more goresome than called for. But seeing I did it for no more than an honest wage, and times being hard like they were, he reckoned I wasn't much a bad sort all over.

"Ain't there no thing you can do for me then?" I liked to know.

This Rhadamanthus scratches his horns and says, "Rules is rules, I'm afraid. But what I've leave to do is, I can let you choose any part of hell you like—which if a man is wrong in the head in the right ways, can be sorta fun if he knows how."

So I picked where the lusty lady demons stand naked on a table a-front of you and cover each other in butter, and lick the butter off each other, and moan as the other licks the butter off. If you so much as touch them, they put a spear through your head. And if you touch yourself, they put a spear through that too. Well, beats boiling in pitch, I figure, and at least I get to sit and don't have to push no boulders. Plus, spears suit me 'cause my head's already nothing to look at. So we agreed to it, Rhaddy and me. There, that settled.

"Oh, and one more thing," he says. "Your many and colorsome sins have scintillated this court more than most, so in recompense, see if this don't suit you also. I can send your shade back to earth to witness a revenge for your gruesome end. Not that hell will intervene against your malefactors any, but seeing as their desert's already forthcoming, you may as well savor of it what you can."
    (Rubbing his hands together)
Now, me, not one to hold grudges, but I do love a good show.
    (Glancing back at the stage)
So that's what you and I just had relish to view of. How 'bout it, then? The best bit's how everyone got their fill what's coming to 'em.

rhadamanthus

    (Whispering)
Though none of it was pie, the dessert I like best.

Ol' Humphrey got it worst, it seems. Him's the one I fault most for my head, anyway. Giving that kid a piece and telling 'im to sort us in that little room, it's a wonder we didn't all lose our faces.

Next, the kid himself. Sure, for now he's gonna be Chief Intend-Ent of the Botanists and ruler of all Dodoville. But they say the higher ya rise, the harder ya fall, and you don't need no necromancin' to know *that'll* never last. Botanocracy! Thirty-forty years from now, people'll ask how such a thing came to pass.

And Daggett. Well, what you don't know is, before she died, Mara'd been bastin' my kabab every Tuesday behind Marty's Camel-back Caramel Custards—in exchange for me having re-hinged her last agent's elbows—and I've never met a girl who lapped the gravy like her, so I was really cross when she was lost at sea. Now, if justice was poetical, Daggett'd be the one choked dead with a big, throbby eel down the throat—to make up for me no longer getting my mutton swallowed—but I guess what happens after Daggett left the theater is revenge enough for me.
    (The idea striking him)
Christ's crotch-rag! I forget you living see no more than your eyes can show you.
    (Painting the picture with his hands)
Okay, so as I speak, his car races the winding road up Mount Myrtle, to find the hardy flower rootin' atop the rim with power to neutralize any poison. Of course, you can't just eat 'em, the petals have to dry in the sun for three days, then to extract the anti-venom you have to—Listen, I'm no Bunsen, but let's just say it's a fool's errand.

Anyhow, his eyes get harder and harder to focus with the poison workin' intra his venouses. The sight-image in his brain starts to gray and crack, his hands lay mud-heavy upon the wheel. Fear settles in, the frosty finger of death tickle-creeps up over his shoulder. He thinks, "Why did I not kill that Flynn when I had the chance? Nothing'd be more satisfying than to reach down inside him and pull his liver out his big beefhole."

Well, that's just how I'd do it. They don't call me Noodle for nothing.

Annnnd there he goes, whoop, off the cliff. The car pitches forward and—ooh, that'll sting! Ah, the engine's caught fire! Flames creepin' now toward the gas tank. Daggett struggles to push out the door, but his strength is fading inside the crumpled steel. His body shudders, preparing to sunder his soul unto hell.

But first, what's this? In a voice incredibly faint, he repeats a single word. Ho, a prayer? to whatever mountain nymph or dryad might happen to hear? Over and over. Listen now. Halp. Haaaaaalp. Halp me!
  (Giddy as a schoolboy)
Naw, just shittin'. He died on impact.
  (Brushing his hands off)
Well, that about rounds it off. Time to go try not to get speared through the head, ha ha! Except for when it's really worth it, know what I'm saying?
  (Makes a rude gesture)
Good night!

  (Exits.)

(LIGHTS UP)

ABOUT the author

WILL MADDEN is a native of the Bronx, NY. He studied Greek and Latin literature at the University of Pennsylvania. Primarily a novelist, he has written genre stories such as Kevin The Vampire, The Killbug Eulogies, and Sky Joust: The Purple Onion vs. The Pestilence, which also takes place in the world of this play. His hobbies include studying languages and card magic. All his children are pets, and all his pets are house plants. He currently resides in Washington, DC. Contact him @silverstrigil or at silverstrigil.net.

If he could appear to you as a space hologram and beseech you for one thing, it'd be that you go online and review this book at your favorite online bookseller. He has no idea how to beseech something more earnestly than in hologram form.

www.ingramcontent.com/pod-product-compliance
Lightning Source LLC
Chambersburg PA
CBHW070424010526
44118CB00014B/1887